Enneagram and Chakras

Chakras

Define Different Personalities and Human Behavior to Discover Your Own Self

(Complete Guide to Test and Understand Personality Types)

Gerardo Gantz

Published by Knowledge Icons

Gerardo Gantz

All Rights Reserved

Enneagram and Chakras: Define Different Personalities and Human Behavior to Discover Your Own Self (Complete Guide to Test and Understand Personality Types)

ISBN 978-1-990084-59-1

LEGAL & DISCLAIMER

Table of Contents

Introduction

The following chapters will discuss a history of the Enneagram symbol, its relevance to Christianity, a description of each of the types, and an eclectic methodology to help you unlock the meaning of each of the personality types in order to increase self-awareness and improve your interpersonal and inner life.

There are plenty of books on this subject on the market, thanks again for choosing this one! Every effort was made to ensure it is full of as much useful information as possible, please enjoy!

Chapter 1: The Enneagram

The Enneagram is a system of personality types based on nine different types of personalities–with the theory that all fall into one of these nine categories. Many claim it's an old system with Sufism roots, and others believe it's much newer. But, it's a more complex system that meets the eye at first sight.

It is our childhood personality that we create in order to deal with our own personal climate. The Enneagram identifies nine distinctive patterns, but it also explains how each of the nine personalities shifts under pressure and also when we feel completely healthy.

So why would we like to label anybody as a particular type of person? Okay, while we can go to the moon, most of us have tremendous difficulty understanding each other. A key to understanding others is first to develop a proper understanding of ourselves and to look at ourselves through the Enneagram.

It's not an easy thing to microscope your own personality. You must be prepared to hear and discover things you don't really want to know about yourself. Some of the things you discover may not please you. It does not matter to find out anything about yourself if you're not prepared to address the results, and it takes time, work, and a lot of commitment to change your behavior.

There are a few points you have to remember when using Enneagram: firstly, we need to realize that all types of personality are essentially positive. Secondly, you should be very careful about "typing" somebody else, i.e., putting somebody into a specific Enneagram class.

Understanding where another person sits on the nine points will definitely lead to better understanding and interaction. But the downside is that it can also lead to stereotyping people and can lead to certain people associating specific

3

negative reactions. For example, we risk assuming that because someone is a type 7, they're unengaged and will always be. Or if they're a type 9, they're going to be lazy. We impose our own prejudiced ideas by stereotyping people and trying to forecast their reactions, and that is not a good thing.

As we shall see, each of the nine personality types has positive and negative characteristics. This is perfectly meaningful because no human being is perfect, but it is not healthy to focus on negative aspects of the character of someone. Acceptance for people who they are and not what we want them to lead to better communication and better human relationships.

What does the Enneagram mean, in fact?

Broken down, the words Ennea and Gram mean, respectively, "nine" and "pattern." So what are the nine types of personalities? You can have a much greater understanding of the reactions of other individuals if you know your own kind, but the underlying classifications are essentially the same as the

Peacemaker/Mediator

The Perfectionist/Reformer

The Observer

The Tragic Romantic

The Trooper

The Performer/Achiever

Confronter/The Boss

The Giver/Helper

Dreamer/The Epicure

It will become easier to motivate yourself to achieve things in life if you understand the drivers to your own conduct. Followers of the Enneagram agree that everyone has a primary driver that defines our emotions, feelings, and actions to a large degree.

This catalyst or passion provides the concept or view of life for an individual. Passion has a negative label, but it does not indicate that the type of personality is negative. It means that personality is largely dependent on this particular behavior. But it is the raw material—all personality types can make this "negative" positive with work, self-examination, and understanding.

For example, the giver believes that everybody needs assistance, type 2. The motivation behind this is pride. Type 2 is proud to say that it can help everyone to build an inflated sense of self-worth. But by looking at and recognizing this life inspiration, it can turn this pride into humility and make better use of its natural gift to help people.

The driver behind type 9 is slothful, i.e., lazy about life. Decisions take energy because both sides of the argument have to be weighed up, so it is easier to ignore difficulty and wait for it to be gone or for anyone else to solve it. Above all else, Nines value harmony. If this driver is not known, they will spend their lives avoiding disagreements or claims.

Nonetheless, Nines, like all other forms of personalities, can be good for the world.

Once they realize that their underlying motivation is slothful, they can improve their performance by setting small goals and structuring processes. An innate desire to avoid disputes allows them to establish a highly useful psychological isolation in volatile situations.

It is very important to realize that everyone has only one kind-you can't be a two-camp leader! Some people, particularly those who have just begun to study the Enneagram, believe that they are a mix of the various characteristics. They identify features that seem to support this theory. Our personal features are not the same as our motivation behind them. We can have similar features and responses to other people but are totally different forms of personality.

It can be hard to classify yourself as a certain type. We all have a picture of who we are instead of knowing who we are. It may be helpful to ask a close friend, who you trust 100%, to give you your personality input. Be alert. However, that kind of integrity can not survive in all relationships! And note that every type of personality has both positive and negative aspects. Don't get the negatives hung up. Alternatively, put your energy into improving the character's positive aspects.

Enneagram and Your Inner Motivation

The Helper, The Reformer, The Individualist, The Achiever, The Enthusiast, The Loyalist, The Peacemaker, The Challenger, The Observer.

Hello to a new personality view! A basic but insightful model for the types of human personalities, the Enneagram will help you find what really leads you and everybody else you meet in life and how to make the most of this knowledge.

You will gain a lot from understanding your guy and others around you, rather than just saying... Find out what your personality's color is. You can get a good insight into yourself with Enneagram and find out what really motivates you in the heart. Discover your passion again.

Take a moment to consider... Would job sound like torture, and are you running like a zombie during your days? Wake up, work, come late and fatigued home, maybe grumpy— rinse and repeat on the pillow. Okay, perhaps the answer is simple: if your work does not satisfy your desire inside, it will never make you feel very happy. You just pass through the motions.

Or if you have a great job, and would just like to understand better people, like your boyfriend, or a still girl who won't leave the corner or even a boring man who isn't going to stop praising, Enneagram will allow you to look at things from your point of view. You will learn how to get along with other people, their compatibility, and even what they think of you. Know what makes them happy, and you happy yourself.

And I promise you, and it will be just as fun to find out if not more, what color your personality is.

Below is a quick overview of all nine types of personalities: Type 1— The Reformer / The Perfectionist Reformers live up to high standards since they always seek and do everything correctly. They are the most reliable people, fair and honest, who hold principles and ethics firmly to your feet. They are always realistic and reasonable, but they are far from being an idle dreamer. Perfectionists want to avoid wrath and errors in life.

Type 2— Everyone wants to be accepted, valued, and wanted — helpers make it an element of life. They try to do this by planning a positive and warm presence and looking for the needs of the people around them. As a result, many people want to have them around. Helpers want a poor impression to avoid.

Type 3— The motivation of Achievers is positive and efficient, all that they do revolves around these objectives. Often optimistic, they are all they seem to be and tend to be role models that inspire others. It abhors defeat and does its best to avoid it.

Form 4-The Individualist Individualists live at the very edge of true and creative lives. They seem to almost fade in and out between the two, always comparing what they have and what they want (but most of the time, can't). Individualists are inspired to pursue the true meaning of life, to explore themselves, to look for things in life, not simply to be another eye. I want to be famous because these people are different... So you know that better.

Form 5–Observers like to explore their different interests and ideas alone. We are driven by the deep need to learn, understand, and be self-sufficient. Observers wish to control them for themselves and only for themselves, not others-making them the ultimate independents. They try to avoid being foolish or dumb.

Type 6–The loyalist loyalists are mainly seeking a sense of security. Loyalist comes in many varieties, from the elderly and steep to the audacious and confrontational. Two styles of Sixes exist phobias and counter-phobia. The former appears terrified and seeks acceptance. The latter is fighting their fear, seeming frightened and blunt — all emphasis on coping with anxiety.

Type 7-Enthusiast You are most definitely seven— enthusiastic— if you have no age, always springy, always engaged, and always busy. Enthusiasts are motivated by the fact that they are happy and have fun, contribute to the world, and reduce pain and suffering.

Type 8–Challenger The first word in mind to describe people of this type should be "strong," as challengers are strong and self-sufficient and aspire to be. They want to stop being called poor... And the people who think they're going to get what's coming to them very quickly, anyway.

Type 9-The Peacemaker The Peacemakers are simply adaptable and neutral, as they need to remain in peace and merge with others and avoid conflict. Since they are so adaptable, the other eight types around them influence them significantly. As a result, a wide range of Peacemakers exists, from those with delicate, gentle personalities to powerful, independent people.

So, what kind do you think you're?

If you are interested in reading more, such as personality tests, short and realistic, or the long and scientifically sound, real-life examples of all types, the three primary motivations of self-image, fear, frustration, and tips from the best books of the Enneagram.

The Types of Enneagram Personality

The Perfectionist

These would be people who need to work. Serious, idealistic, and judgmental are typically perfectionists. Decisions are taken with the' one correct way' in mind. Their work is designed to reflect extremely high standards. They teach, preach, and monitor others continuously. This causes others to feel caught or dismissed. The fiercest perfectionist anger is directed at itself. Perfectionists are frank, idealistic, and visionaries at their best. You have a clear vision of what to do with the ability to lead others.

The Helper

Helper strives to be valued. They give with the intention of mutual thankfulness. Helpers are psychologically seductive in their relationship. Nice and manipulative, helpers are important and cute to others. This is their way of influencing and seeking power. Helpers have impeccable emotions, desires, and appetites for others. We are highly compassionate and professional in their customer services. Helpers serve and make others the best.

The Producer

The manufacturers are more than likely employees. They are applauded for the work they have done. Manufacturers can be high performers, motivated, and competitive. They must be honored for their successes. Some people could say that producer is involved in themselves and obsessed with image. They are shallow, superficial, unrealistic, and appropriate. Manufacturers are often only seen as their description. Among their best producers, successful leaders are willing to solve problems and influence others.

The Connoisseur

It is easy for a Knower to move towards the beautiful, genuine, true, and unusual. Such men are melancholic and sentimental. Knowers show impeccable taste in their concerns. They seek deeper significance below the surface. Feelings are the driving force behind their decisions. Knower seems to be pleased with the impeccable. They can look noisy or snooty. We are imaginative and conceivable at their best. Knowers love the world's attractiveness, taste, and elegance.

The Sages

pursue control of their particular fields. They are unconnected emotionally. It is said that the wise watch the world from safe points of view. You can store facts, hypotheses, and knowledge here. Sages do not depend on relationships but instead, hide and minimize their needs. Some see them as emotionally detached, hiding behind anything they can find. Sages are at best sensitive, creative, polite, hard-working businessmen — many wizards and dedicated to their fields.

TROUBLESHOOTER

At all, the Troubleshooter Paranoid is concerned with troubling case scenarios. Confidence is a huge issue. They're over-prepared and concerned with what might go wrong. Others may consider their pause frustrating. Troubleshooters can be trustworthy, imaginative, original, intuitive, committed, delicate, and brave. You are known for defending your friends, your boss, and yourself. Troubleshooters are useful to point out slips and hidden motives on the way.

The visionaries

visionary remains positive, and all options remain open. They engage, plan, and have energy-intensive romances. It is difficult for visionaries to grow up. We were regarded as Peter Pans shallow. Visionaries can not easily find risks. Consequently, pain, confrontation, regular responsibilities, and daily work are avoided. Although they make progress, they often fail to do so. The best viewers are talented, witty, inspiring, and lovely. Their ideas and enthusiasm are attractive to people.

The Top Dog

Power and Control are what top dogs are looking for. We openly and loudly express their feelings. Top dogs are described as dominant and stupid. We try confrontations openly and believe that reality always falls into a fight. They focus on their own powers and other weaknesses. Others may be repelled by their flamboyant intimidation. When times, top dogs protect the underdogs they are responsible for.

The mediators

mediators aim to incorporate both individuals and perspectives. Such people easily compromise. You can see other people's feelings, needs, and enthusiasm. Others might consider mediators negligent or spatial. Mediators lead at their best by inspiring others. They are hot, open-hearted people. Mediators are naturally in contact with the group's flow. Mediators are, therefore, great negotiators, team leaders, and border crossings.

Chapter 2: Enneagram And Self-Discovery

The Enneagram personality type system is very dynamic and enlightening. We all tend to gravitate towards one of the dominant personality types. If you understand yourself, then you can begin to understand how your character traits affect your life. Once you know this, you can then make the necessary changes to achieve your goals in life. When you start to learn more about these nine personality types, you will begin to see specific patterns in which you have been living all this while. The first step is to explore each of these personality types so that you know the kind that suits you. In the journey towards self-discovery, the first step is awareness. When you become aware of your behavior, you can start to make changes consistently. So, let us learn a little more about all these personality types.

Type 1: The Perfectionist

Type One is known as the Perfectionist or the Reformer. Believe it or not, this personality type tends to be harder on themselves than anyone else around them. They often tend to be quite critical of themselves and their inner critic never takes a rest. At times, they can be wise and discerning. However, they are demanding and nit-picking. Type Ones often strive to achieve perfection that is somehow always out of their reach. They not only have high standards for themselves but others as well. They want to do the right thing and are quite responsible; this makes them the ideal employee.

Not just that, they tend to have impossibly high moral standards. In fact, they are an excellent example of what integrity and ethics should look like. Well, the world of politics can certainly use more Ones.

They might strive for perfection, but this doesn't make them fearless. They fear to be wrong. The need to be right and to do good is quite an endearing trait of the

Ones. At their best, they are rational, principled, idealistic, and productive. They are reform-minded and continuously think of ways in which they can improve themselves. They have the mindset of a perfectionist. They are quite orderly and emotionally constrained. At their worst, they are inflexible, extremely judgmental (of themselves and others alike), hypocritical, and even self-righteous. Ones believe that they are objective and reasonable, regardless of what others think of them.

Critical motivators for Ones include living up to their own high standards, excelling in everything that they do, and being efficient. They want to be fair in all their dealings, and they honestly want to make the world a better place to live in.

This personality type does sound too good to be true, doesn't it? The attributes that are favorable for them are also the ones that hinder their growth in life. It is quite likely that famous celebrities like Al Gore, Gandhi, Hillary Clinton, Jerry Brown,

21

Margaret Thatcher, Joan Baez, Katherine Hepburn, Bill Moyers, Martha Stewart, Thomas Jefferson, Ralph Nader, Sandra Day O'Connor, and Kenneth Starr are all Type One personalities.

My message to all the Ones out there is that you are okay if you do what you think is right. Having high standards for yourself and others is okay. However, you might not even realize that this attitude can cause you lots of problems. In fact, you can solve half of your troubles if you just cut yourself some slack. Give yourself a break, and give others a break. Everyone deserves it.

Type 2: The Helper

Type Two, or the Helpers, as their name suggests, are quite good at giving, but not so much at receiving. They are generous and always want to help others. There is a reason why they like to help others; it makes them feel like they are needed. They like to be required. People are drawn to all Twos like bees to honey because of their generous and helpful nature. They can do things for others without any expectations. They make excellent counselors. A person with this personality type can open up your heart because their heart is already open to the world. They can see the good in others.

There are three major things that all Twos believe. They believe that they should place the needs of others before their own. They should always give if they want to receive something. The third belief is that they must always work hard to earn the affection of others. These are the three beliefs that all the Twos firmly believe. In fact, these are the opinions they have held since their childhood. If you notice that you share these three beliefs, it is quite likely that you are a Two. Twos feel that it is selfish to have needs of their own. Well, that sounds kind of sad, doesn't it? The funny thing is, they aren't entirely selfless. They do have needs and expectations, but they are scared to acknowledge their needs. Melanie Hamilton from Gone with the Wind does seem like a perfect Type Two personality.

Their primary fear is that they are unloved or unwanted. They cannot stand the thought of not being loved by others. Since Twos like to feel needed, they never want to feel unwanted. They have an intense desire to feel loved. At their best, Twos are quite empathetic, concerned, nurturing, and loving. At their worst, Twos are quite possessive and manipulating. Their domineering nature can be quite a turn-off. They might not even realize that they are manipulative or any such thing. They believe that they are caring and loving people and they are, up to a certain extent.

The key motivating factors for Twos are that they want to give and receive unconditional love. The thought of being loved and accepted motivates them to do better. Famous personalities like Eleanor Roosevelt, Barbara Bush, Bishop Desmond Tutu, Albert Schweitzer, Leo Buscaglia, Jr., Ann Landers, Sammy Davis, Nancy Reagan, John Denver, Dolly Parton, Florence Nightingale, and Luciano Pavarotti are likely number Twos.

My message to all the Twos out there is that it is okay to let others love you. You don't always have to do something to feel loved. It is okay to receive even without giving at times. Learn to be a gracious receiver. You must understand the difference between loving and needing. Love and need are different; the sooner you know the difference, the more liberated you will feel. Having expectations is okay. In fact, you should acknowledge your expectations. No one is a mind reader, and at times you will have to spell out what you want from people. It doesn't make you selfish or shallow. So please stop thinking that.

Type 3: The Achiever

Type Three consists of all the go-getters and performers. They like to develop themselves and others around them. In comparison to other personality types, Type Threes get immense pleasure when they attain their goals. They are often successful and can motivate themselves to achieve their goals. The personal definition of success for Threes depends on their family lives, culture, and their social values. For some, a large home can signify success, for others it might be a good education, so on and so forth. Regardless of their definition of success, Threes want their family and community to view them as a success. Threes are therefore almost always goal-oriented in life. They often behave in a manner that will help them get the attention and praise they crave. In their childhood, Threes spend a lot of their time and energy on activities that are of value to their family members and peers. Their quotient of self-worth depends on other's definition of success. Without success, they will feel quite empty. Do you remember Don Dapper from Mad Men? He is the embodiment of a type Three personality.

The primary fear of all the Threes is a feeling of worthlessness. They dread to think of their lives without the success that they hold dear to their heart. Their primary desire is to feel worthy and valuable. They are authentic, self-assured, motivated, and focused at their best. At their absolute worst, they can be quite pretentious, calculating, and even deceptive. They like to achieve success; the means don't always matter. They want to believe that they are outstanding. However, it is wrong when they think that they will be successful only if others believe that they are successful.

The key motivators for Threes are the goals they set for themselves. They want to become visible and famous. Success is everything to them. Eminent personalities like Bill Clinton, Oprah Winfrey, Paul McCartney, Tom Cruise, Barbra Streisand, Michael Jordan, Shirley MacLaine, Denzel Washington, Tiger Woods, and John Edwards are most likely all Threes.

My message to all the Threes out there is that you shouldn't let others determine your worth. Don't believe that you aren't successful until someone says otherwise. You are good the way you are. You should do things that make you feel happy. Don't do them because others think it's cool.

You can never find true happiness if you let others decide what is good or bad. You can choose for yourself and have some faith in yourself. Don't live your life according to the expectations of others. Take some time and think about the things you like and the things you want. Without your success, who are you?

Type 4: The Individualist

Type Four, known as the Individualist, or the Romantic, are undoubtedly perfect for romantic relationships. Type Four consists of all those who give priority to their relationships over everything else in their lives. Regardless of whether Fours are single or in a relationship, they dedicate most of their energy towards their relationships. If you want to know if you are a Four, then you should analyze your childhood. Fours try to build their identity around how different they are from everyone else.

Have you ever wondered if you were probably switched at birth? As funny as it sounds, Romantics often like to think that they were. Fours often feel that their parents never understood their "real persona." Not just that, they often feel misunderstood by their families. Fours tend to think that there is something wrong with them and this starts their lifelong quest to find their true identity. They tend to focus on all those things that they think are missing in their relationships. Instead of feeling grateful for the things that do go right, they search for things that don't seem right to them. Fours tend to doubt their identity, and it makes them appear mysterious and intriguing to others. They hope that they will find someone who will love them for who they are. Well, that does sound quite confusing. How can anyone love you for who you are if you aren't sure of it yourself?

The primary fear that all those who possess this personality type harbor is that they don't have an identity of their own and that they aren't of any significance. They desire to express themselves and create an identity for themselves. Fours are quite compassionate, creative, sensitive, and imaginative. At their absolute worst, they seem withdrawn, melancholic, and even self-absorbed. Often, people think that Fours are moody and like to alienate themselves from others. Fours want to believe that they are unique.

One thing motivates Fours more than anything else in their quest to understand themselves: Fours constantly try to "find" themselves. Famous personalities who seem like Type Fours are Tennessee Williams, Cher, Bob Dylan, Ingmar Bergman, Soren Kierkegaard, Rudolph Nureyev, Judy Garland, Maria Callas, Edgar Allen Poe, Jeremy Irons, James Dean, Frederic Chopin, and Paul Simon.

My message to all the Fours out there is that you should let go of your imaginary self-image and should instead express yourself to others. No one will understand you if you don't try to express yourself. Accept your flaws and realize that there is nothing wrong with you. Flaws make us human, and if you have flaws, it merely means that you are human too! Learn to see who you are and accept yourself. You cannot find true love if you don't love yourself.

Type 5: The Observer

Type Fives are among the most elusive personality types and are known as the Investigators. Most Fives don't like the limelight, and they are instead happy to stay on the sidelines. They want to immerse themselves in their world of observations, and they gain confidence when they can internalize the knowledge they gain. They like to know how the world works. In short, they like to observe more than anything else. Fives have an inherent thirst for knowledge, and they want to know it all. They tend to use their relentless pursuit of knowledge to mask their insecurities.

Fives often think that they don't possess the ability to do things as well as others. Instead of trying to do something to rectify this situation, Fives tend to withdraw into their minds, their haven. They like their shell, and it gives them a sense of security and stability. Fives are often drawn to things that are somewhat unusual, less explored, and even unthinkable. Familiarity doesn't comfort them.

In your childhood, did you not feel safe in your home? No, not that you had an abusive childhood or anything of that sort. But did your parents overwhelm you? Did you feel the need to retreat into your private space? Did you, and do you, still spend a lot of time immersed in your imaginary world? A world that's full of books, music, and computers? If yes, then it is quite likely that you are a Five. Fives don't fall into what others perceive to be "normal." They define their world, and they are quite happy in it. They want to create their niche where they can be independent and confident.

The primary fear that all Fives have is that they cannot do things and that they are incompetent. Their fundamental desire is to be capable and competent in life. At their best, all Fives are quite perceptive, curious, and inventive. They are often thought of as intellectuals and intense. At their absolute worst, Fives can be detached, cynical, eccentric, and even abrasive.

Key motivations in life for Fives are the desire to control their environment with understanding, to prevent the intrusion of others, and to have the intellect and the security they desire. Albert Einstein, Vincent Van Gogh, Georgia O'Keefe, Stephen Hawking, Bill Gates, Isaac Asimov, Stanley Kubrick, Emily Dickenson, James Joyce, John Lennon, Jane Goodall, Bobby Fischer, Frederick Nietzsche, Lily Tomlin, and Stephen King all seem like Type Fives.

My message to all the Fives is that it is time you step into the real world. Don't ignore other things in your pursuit of knowledge. You don't have to retreat into your mind to escape the world. Learn to become engaged in your life and live your life. If you don't take any action, you cannot obtain any results. There is so much more to life than the world you have created for yourself. Don't run away from things, and learn to face them instead. Fives possess great intellect. Instead of being observers all the time, you should take action. Don't withdraw yourself from reality. However, it doesn't mean that the world doesn't need any Fives. Where would we all be without the discoveries and inventions of great scientists?

Type 6: The Loyalist

Type Six personalities often tend to have a down to earth approach towards life. They are a breath of fresh air when compared to all the lofty and idealistic views that other personality types tend to hold about life. They value safety and security more than anything else. Sixes are loyal friends. Not just that, they are loyal to their beliefs as well. Once they make up their mind about something and they believe in it, they will defend their belief at all costs. They are loyal to others, and they expect the same in return. They might seem brave on the exterior, but they lack self-confidence when they are no longer in their comfort zone.

Do you spend a lot of time thinking about the challenges that life throws your way? Do you fear to make big decisions by yourself? Do you usually depend on others for guidance? At the same time, do you hate it when others make decisions for you? You don't like to let others take the reins of your life, do you? If yes, then you indeed are a Six. Sixes like their security and safety. If they fail to create this, they tend to become anxious.

The underlying fear that plagues this personality type is that they will be left without any support or guidance. Sixes like their support system and it is all that they desire. At their best, all Sixes are quite confident, courageous, committed, and reliable. The traits that are usually associated with a Six are loyal (duh!), anxious, and dutiful. At their worst, this type can be very confused, indecisive, defensive, and submissive as well. You need to believe that you are a dependable and a committed person; only then will others think the same.

A couple of things that seem to motivate this personality type is their desire to be liked, their need to follow the rules, and the approval of others. Robert F. Kennedy, Tom Hanks, Malcolm X, Richard Nixon, George H.W. Bush, Bruce Springsteen Princess Diana, Richard Cheney, Woody Allen, Julia Roberts, Diane Keaton, and Gloria Steinem seem like likely candidates for this type of personality.

My advice to all the Sixes out there is that you should let go of all the anxieties you harbor. The world isn't as bad as you seem to think. Let go of all the ambivalences you nurture. You like it when others support you. However, at the same time, you are put off when others get too involved in your life. You enjoy your space, and it is okay. You should learn to draw a line between comfort and stress. Learn to express yourself. It is the only way in which you can get what you want. Learn to trust yourself. Listen to your gut and don't ignore it. It is better to depend on yourself than others.

Type 7: The Enthusiast

The Type Seven, or the Enthusiast is the busy and fun-loving type of personality. They are quite spontaneous and versatile. You can never take a Seven's sense of adventure. These optimistic souls approach life with a sense of curiosity. Everything seems to fascinate them. These fun-loving and playful personalities are like a breath of fresh air. They are always up for an adventure. Do you have that one friend who is always up for any random plan, from going on an exotic vacation to shopping at Target! They are pretty much up for anything, and their enthusiasm levels don't seem to diminish. Are you that friend? Boredom is a word that isn't familiar to Sevens. Variety and activity help them to escape the clutches of the mundane life that most of us seem to be trapped in.

Sevens' thought processes are anticipatory—they foresee events and come up with ideas on the go; they favor activities that stimulate their mind, and this, in turn, gives them more things to think about. Well, this is a never-ending cycle. The rush of a new idea is quite thrilling for Sevens. They are happy when they can be spontaneous. Instead of spending a lot of time on one task or thought, they will instead do multiple things. Sevens experience anxiety when they aren't in touch with their inner voice that guides them.

To cope with the stress they feel, they will try to do different things to distract their minds, and it means that they have more negative feelings due to their detachment from their consciousness. Sigh! Being a Seven might be exhausting. All their energy and enthusiasm cannot do them any good if they are not in touch with their consciousness. They crave stimulation, they thrive when there is change, and they need to be on the move, always. They can keep up with a ton of activity that would otherwise exhaust the other personality types. Sevens are full of energy, and they don't like it when others feel low. They tend to go out of their way to cheer others up. They are the sorts who will happily turn the lemons into lemonade and do it with a smile.

During their childhood, most o Sevens tend to feel that they need to take care of themselves. It doesn't mean that their parents or primary caregivers were negligent. It merely says that due to certain situations, Sevens believe that they need to nurture themselves. As they start to become independent, Sevens tend to focus on transitional objects. Transitional objects is the term that psychologists use to describe things that serve as distractions to cope with anxiety. Sevens try hard to find transitional objects so that they don't have to deal with any emotional conflicts or fears.

The primary fear that all Sevens harbor is the feeling of being trapped. They fear that they will be stuck in pain and deprivation. Their primary desire is to feel content and to fulfill all their needs. A

Seven at their best is enthusiastic, acquisitive, and energetic. Their love for transitional objects makes them seem somewhat materialistic and excessive. At their worst, they can be impulsive, erratic, and manic too. Stop thinking that something is wrong in the present moment. If you feel as if something is wrong, maybe you should spend some time and try to analyze the situation to find out the cause of anxiety that you experience.

The one thing that motivates a Seven more than anything else is a sense of freedom to live without any obligations or constraints. Sevens want to have fun and experience life to the fullest. All their actions boil down to these motivational factors. Famous personalities like Robin Williams, Bette Midler, John F. Kennedy, Steven Spielberg, Mozart, Lauren Bacall, Goldie Hawn, Federico Fellini, Jim Carrey, Benjamin Franklin, Elizabeth Taylor, Jack Nicholson, Lucille Ball, and Mick Jagger are perfect candidates for the type Seven personality.

My message to all the Sevens is to slow down for a while. There is no rush, and you don't have to be on the move all the time. Take some time and learn to connect with your inner self. Learn to enjoy the moment instead of thinking about all sorts of distractions. It is okay to stay still for a while and learn to make your peace with life. You can make better use of energy if you can focus. Practice meditation to gain control of your thoughts. You should control your thoughts, and it should never be the other way around.

Type 8: The Challenger

Type Eights are quite intense and expressive. Even Fours are intense and passionate, but they tend to be more sensitive and emotional about it. However, Eights can be very direct and powerful. Eights are quite a challenge. As their name suggests, they love lively discussions and thrive when they have to overcome a problem. They never shy away from a confrontation and meet it head-on. Type Eights are powerful, almost dominating, confident, decisive, willful, and slightly confrontational. They love challenges and view them as an opportunity to improve themselves. They are very charismatic and have the psychological ability to sway others to follow them. Eights are honest, open, and straightforward. They value their independence and love to make decisions on their own.

The willpower and energy that Eights possess are infectious. At an early age, Eights learn to develop their strength, will, and the endurance necessary to survive in this world. Eights don't like to be controlled by others, and they don't appreciate the thought that someone can have power over them. They are the captain of their ship, and they will not like it any other way. They are proud individualists. Eights might seem quite tough on the surface, but they are human too. They feel hurt and experience rejection like all of us. The only difference is that they will never speak about their vulnerabilities. They don't just avoid talking about their vulnerabilities; they won't even like to accept their vulnerabilities. It means that they have a little trouble receiving and giving love.

Most Eights seem to take on the role of an adult quite early in their life. They realize that it is not a good thing to be gentle in this unmerciful world. Their outlook towards life is quite bleak. They are always on their guard. They do not like to let their guard down, because if they do, they become vulnerable. Do you remember Tony Soprano from The Sopranos? Well, he is the perfect example of this personality type.

The primary fear that all Eights harbor is of being controlled and betrayed. They like to protect themselves and their independence. They have a strong sense of self-preservation. At their best, they are courageous, heroic, and resourceful. However, their best traits become their shortcomings eventually. At their worst, they can be dictatorial and hard-hearted. Often, they come across as bullies.

The things that motivate them are their desire to protect the weak, to have control over their life, and their will to wield power.

Famous personalities like Martin Luther King, Jr., Mikhail Gorbachev, Franklin D. Roosevelt, Sean Connery, Lyndon Johnson, Indira Gandhi, Nelson Mandela, Anwar Sadat, Toni Morrison, Barbara Walters, Susan Sarandon, Golda Meier, Pablo Picasso, and Frank Sinatra seem to possess all the traits of a Type Eight personality.

My message to all the Eights is to open themselves up. Being soft and gentle is okay. It doesn't mean that you are weak. There is nothing wrong with being vulnerable. There is nothing more beautiful than opening up to another person. Learn to trust others a little. Letting others in is okay. Getting hurt is a part of life, of growing up. You don't have to worry about control all the time. Trust that you have a role to play in life.

Type 9: The Mediator

The final personality type in the Enneagram is that of a Mediator or Peacemaker. This personality type encompasses all the other categories. They can have the strength of Eight, the enthusiasm and energy of a Seven, the dutifulness of a Six, the intellect of a Five, the creativity of a Four, a Three's will to achieve, the generosity of a Two, and the idealism of a One. It is quite tricky for Nines to determine their personality since they feel that they can relate to all the personality types in the Enneagram. They are so empathetic that they have a tough time differentiating their feelings from those of others.

Nines often crave a stronger identity of their own. The best profession that is suited for Nines is that of a counselor. Nines are receptive, agreeable, and complacent. They are known as Peacemakers because they spend most of their time achieving internal and external peace. They love harmony more than anything else.

The basic fear of a Peacemaker is separation and loss. Nines crave peace of mind and a sense of wholeness. At their best, they are accepting, good-natured, and extremely reassuring. The adjectives that describe this type the best are complacent, compliant, and self-effacing. They might come across as slightly disengaged from time to time. The negative traits of this personality type are that they can be passive, ineffectual, and even numb. All the Nines out there, you need to understand that you are okay even when others around you aren't. The state of being of others shouldn't bother you to the extent that it disturbs your mental peace. The thing that motivates this personality type is their desire to live in peace and harmony with others. Abraham Lincoln, Walt Disney, Carl Jung, Whoopi Goldberg, Ron Howard, Gerald Ford, George Lucas, Audrey Hepburn, Walter Cronkite, Garrison Keillor, Kevin Costner, Jim Henson, Queen Elizabeth II, and Norman Rockwell are all likely to be Nines.

My message to all the Nines out there is to understand yourself. It is good that you can understand others, but how well do you know yourself? Take some time and think about the feelings you experience and the thoughts that you think. Are these your thoughts and feelings or are these the reflections of those around you? Your love for peace is terrific, but understand that you cannot bring peace to everyone around you. Learn to be content with yourself. Whenever something bothers you, take a moment to think about whether you can do something about it or not. If you cannot do anything to change the situation, then you shouldn't let it bother you.

Eleven behavior tips for the Nine Enneagram's

If you want to lead a better life, regardless of the Enneagram personality types, here are a couple of things that you can try. Here are the ten behaviors that can help change your life and will make you a happy person.

1.Not everything in your life will go precisely in the manner that you have planned. There will be setbacks. Things happen. You might mess things up. Obsessing too much over things and making your happiness dependent on outcomes will do you no good whatsoever. You need to learn to be happy, come what may. People tend to get in their way. We do this without realizing it. So you need to quit worrying about a specific outcome.

2.Things will happen, and there will be things that are beyond your control. The only thing you control is your actions. You cannot control the situations you are in. You should stop worrying about obtaining a specific result. Instead, concentrate on the manner in which you can make the most of what's given to you. If you try too hard to get a particular result, you will tend to get in your own way. Desperation will not get you the results you want. It will hinder your growth. Stop trying to fit in where you don't belong. If the shoe doesn't fit, it is time to move on. Find something that you are comfortable with.

3.No two human beings are alike. So why should we all have just one standard for measuring success? All of us end up getting stuck in the rat race that the society has created towards achieving the so-called rules of "success" that are set by the community. There will always be someone that's better than you at something. There will never be sufficient time to do everything. Instead, you should focus on the things you opt for.

4.When you select something, you have simultaneously rejected something else. It is the norm of life, and it is entirely all right to do so. It is quite enjoyable to choose what you want to do. You need to define what happiness, success, and wealth mean to you. You cannot let society decide what you need or think you need. If that's the case, then you will always fall short of something or the other. You need to stop comparing yourself to others and stop competing with others. It is the only manner in which you will get ahead in life. Pull yourself out of the endless rat race and the rut you are stuck in.

5.How many times have you told yourself "just this once"? Most of us have convinced ourselves that we are capable of breaking our own rules. We always find reasons to justify these small choices we make. None of these things feel like a significant decision initially. However, over a period, these things end up forming a part of the bigger picture. Human beings are good at sabotaging themselves. People tend to behave in a manner that goes against their goals or their ideals. The gap between what you do and what you should be doing should be as small as possible. The more modest this gap is, the happier you will be in life. Giving 100 percent commitment is more comfortable than giving 98 percent.

6.When you have committed yourself fully to something this means that the decision has already been made. Unless and until you are fully committed to something, you will always end up being a victim of all the external circumstances in life. If you rely on your willpower, it is more likely that you will end up crumbling. You might think that you are doing better than what you are doing. But you needn't rely on your willpower once you have given your 100 percent commitment. Regardless of the circumstances, your decision has been made. It is all about being proactive instead of being reactive.

7.Abundance, and the lack of it, tend to exist simultaneously in our life. It is always our choice which of these things we tend to. When you have decided to focus your energy on what you have in your life instead of focusing on things that are missing, happiness is a straightforward concept. It can be as simple as gratitude that you feel. According to research, there are specific physical, psychological, and social benefits of feeling gratitude. These benefits include a stronger immune system, reduction in body aches and pains, better blood pressure, and better sleep too. The psychological benefits are increased feelings of positivity; you'll feel more alert, experience more joy, and be more optimistic.

8.The social benefits are that you will feel more helpful, generous, compassionate, forgiving, outgoing, and less isolated. In spite of all these benefits, most people are usually ungrateful. People tend to focus too much of their time and attention on what they don't have. The grass always does appear to be greener on the other side. If there's one thing that you want, after achieving it, there will be something else. There is no end to this ever-growing list of wants. Life has become a constant race of having the best of things. How can you ever be happy when all you want from life is more things? Take a moment and appreciate what you have.

9.Be conscious of the language that you use. People who are grateful make use of different words like gifts, abundance, blessings, fortune, fortunate, and blessed more frequently. If you start incorporating these words into your daily vocabulary, you will realize that the list of things that you need to be grateful for keeps on increasing. It will allow you to understand and appreciate the abundance that is present all around you. Smile a lot and say thank you when someone does something for you. It could be something as simple as acknowledging someone for holding the door open for you.

10.Giving up on the good we possess to pursue the best in life is a good strategy. There are a lot of things in life that are good, and even great. It doesn't mean that you should do them all. Every day, you are faced with once-in-a-lifetime opportunities.

11.Most people tend to grab onto any great opportunity that comes their way, even though it is not in synchronicity with their vision in life. It is the reason why the lives of people tend to move in different directions. They can't move in a single direction on a conscious level. On the contrary, happy people will refuse any opportunity, however incredible it is, as long as they are at peace with themselves. They won't sacrifice their freedom for the sake of security. They won't let distractions divert their attention. There are only specific things in life that can be described as the very "best." You are the only one that gets to decide what's best for you. Don't keep yourself occupied with the so-called "good" activities and miss out on the amazing ones.

Happy people are the ones that live in the present. They don't let go of those moments that matter. They are always grateful for what they have. Happy people focus on those aspects of their life that are significant.

Chapter 3: Historical Development Of Enneagram And What It Portends For Future

Although little has really been said about the origin and meaning of the Enneagram symbol which dates back to as far back as 2500 B.C., its exact origin still remains somewhat uncertain, controversial and cannot be pinpoint to a particular time. Crusaders, Pythagoreans and Neo-Platonists, the Eastern Orthodox Church, Jewish mystics, Sophists, and Sufi mystics are just a few of the sects that have all been linked with the different symbol's discoveries, idea propagation and teachings in one way or the other. Most of those symbols which have been successfully passed down through the ages cannot be fully discussed here in this book. Until very recent times, although somewhat secretly these teachings and symbols of enneagram of personality are passed down through oral tradition of teachings and storytelling.

The philosophical teacher that was also known as a spiritual teacher, George Ivanovic Gurdjieff who lived between 1872-1949 is often regarded as the "very pioneer of the enneagram in the West side of the world," and he is believed to be responsible for the creation of Enneagram diagram that is widely in circulation today. I beseech you to learn more about that wonderful teacher of enneagram personality. However, as it was revealed in the previous chapter of this book, the first known public teachings of the Enneagram of personality and enneagram systems are actually designed, pioneered and championed by the Oscar Ichazo of this word. Ichazo was a South American professor and philosopher who for so many years lectured and wrote many papers on the Enneagram of Personality between the 60s and 70s of the last millennium. The teaching of the Enneagram of Personality and belief system eventually spread, like a wildfire, to academic, spiritual and financial, self-development and growth communities in the US and Bolivia and Chile about that same time in history.

Particularly in the past decades, the Enneagram has seen a tremendous resurgence of widespread interest in both psychological and spiritual circles. It has ties to the Jewish Kabbala and Christianity's seven deadly sins and is seen by some as a precursor to the findings of more modern-day psychologists and behaviorists such as Sigmund Freud, Carl Jung, and Karen Horney.

The Enneagram system that we know today was primarily developed and written over the past 40 years by a handful of dedicated psychologists, academics and students of Ichazo, including Claudio Naranjo. Naranjo was a noted Chilean-born psychiatrist who in turn passed the Enneagram of Personality to other students and to second and third-generation students, several of whom (including Helen Palmer, Robert Ochs, and

Don Richard Riso) provided the foundation for most of the current writings and teachings on the topic.

Teachers of the Enneagram hasten to point out that its basis spiritual and psychological, not scientific. Most also suggest that individuals let their own intuition, skepticism, and logic be their guide in employing those aspects of the Enneagram that they find meaningful, and disregarding the rest.

In his introduction to Personality Types: Using the Enneagram for Self-Discovery, Don Richard Riso articulates the sentiment this way: "In the last analysis, either the descriptions of the personality types in this book have 'the ring of truth' about them or they do not; either the Enneagram makes sense in your own experience or not." It is, according to Riso, the "shock of recognition" that one experiences upon discovering one's own personality type that offers the "most important proof there is of the Enneagram's accuracy."

The Enneagram as a personality barometer and belief system has a long-standing history with its primary image going back a few thousand years in the past. However, in recent times, enneagram has experienced a strong surge and interest amongst some of the world's most successful business moguls, managers, political leaders, religious leaders, spiritual leaders, and entrepreneurs.

Just like Tobi Lutke, the Chief Executive Officer of Shopify mentioned in the conversation he had with Tim Ferris on a particular widely broadcast podcast, that Shopify is so partial to the Enneagram, it has worked very well for them. In the Shopify internal system, he claimed one can see the Enneagram of anybody else as it tells people what it means and what is needed for them to work together without having to hate or fight each other. At Shopify, the idea is to understand and know what areas people have a particular prefixed mindset on and they then try to get them to acquire a growth mindset which can help them become a better human.

Chapter 4: How Do I Find My Enneagram Type?

Like any personality system, the Enneagram has found itself embedded in a plethora of stereotypes.

Fours are creative, yet dramatic. Ones are principled yet judgmental. Sevens are adventurous, yet unreliable while nines are accepting, yet spineless.

Like so many other personality systems, we try to identify ourselves by lining our behaviors up against these stereotypes and determining which ones we most closely resemble. The problem with doing this is that many of us will identify with more than one stereotype.

We're ambitious, but also compassionate. We're creative but also adventurous. We're helpful but also intellectual. We're powerful but also security seeking. We find ourselves lost in a sea of confusion over which type fits us the best of all and too often, we unknowingly place ourselves into the wrong category. This is the problem with using stereotypes to identify one's personality type.

So How Do We Properly Identify Ourselves?

A lesser-known fact about Enneagram is that it isn't meant to be a system that merely identifies clusters of traits. The Enneagram is a dynamic, growth-oriented inventory that aims to pinpoint one's basic fears and motivations, in order to facilitate personal growth through a specific trajectory.

Which traits you utilize – helpfulness, creativity, dutifulness, etc. – are merely manifestations of your basic fears. But which behaviors you employ to escape your fears can be situational.

A type six may tap into their creative side in order to please a mentor – to avoid their basic fear of being without support or guidance – and consequently mistake themselves for a type four. A type three may act dominant and assertive in order to progress professionally and mistake themselves for a type eight. When judging our type based on behavior, we are at a high risk for mistyping ourselves.

The only reliable method of identifying your type is to discover which of the nine basic fears guide the majority of your behavior.

Just as cognitive functions explain the cognitive processes that drive each Myers-Briggs type's behavior, the Enneagram's basic fears identify the driving force between each of the nine type's behaviors.

The nine core fears – as listed in Don Richard Riso and Russ Hudson's "The Wisdom of the Enneagram" are as follows:

Type 1 – The fear of being evil or corrupt.

Type 1s strive to be morally upstanding and virtuous in the face of external corruption. Their pervasive, underlying fear is that they themselves are corrupt, and they must act in a virtuous way in order to prove this fear wrong. Their prime motivation in life is their own sense of integrity. They are constantly aiming to move away from corruption and towards virtue, or the greater good.

Type 2 – The fear of being unloved or unwanted by others.

Type 2s strive to be loved and wanted by those around them. Their pervasive, underlying fear is that there is nothing inherently loveable about them, and they must therefore help others in order to earn their love. Their prime motivation in life is proving themselves worthy of care and love from others. They are constantly aiming to move away from worthlessness and toward relationships that foster mutual loving and caregiving.

Type 3 – The fear of being unaccomplished and worthless.

Type 3s strive to achieve success within their community, believing this to be a measure of their own worth. This type's pervasive, underlying fear is that they are inherently worthless and undesirable apart from their achievements and they must, therefore, accomplish as many things as possible in order to be desired and accepted by others. They are constantly aiming to move away from worthlessness and towards impressive achievements that will earn them the respect and admiration of others.

Type 4 – The fear of lacking a unique, significant identity.

Type 4s strive to prove their uniqueness and individuality to others. Their pervasive, underlying fear is that they would be worthless and unlovable if they were average, therefore they must cultivate as unique an identity as possible in order to prove their own significance. They are constantly aiming to move away from normalcy and toward expressions of intensity and individuality.

Type 5 – The fear of being helpless and inadequate.

Type 5s strive to become as knowledgeable and competent as possible in all of their undertakings. Their pervasive, underlying fear is of being helpless, overwhelmed, and incapable of dealing with the world around them. Therefore, they must learn as much as they can and master as much as they can, in order to reassure themselves that they are competent and capable. They are constantly aiming to move away from ignorance and ambiguity, and toward knowledge and understanding.

Type 6 – The fear of being without support or guidance.

Type 6s strive to find support and guidance from those around them. Their pervasive, underlying fear is that they are incapable of surviving on their own and they must, therefore, seek out as much support and direction from others as much as possible. They are constantly aiming to move away from isolation and towards structure, security, and the guidance of others.

Type 7 – The fear of deprivation and pain.

Type 7s strive to achieve their wildest desires and find fulfillment. Their pervasive, underlying fear is that their needs and desires will not be met by others, and so they must go and pursue them themselves. They are constantly aiming to move away from pain, sadness, and helplessness and towards independence, happiness, and fulfillment.

Type 8 – The fear of being harmed or controlled by others.

Type 8 strives to become strong, independent, and self-directed. Their pervasive, underlying fear is of being violated, betrayed or controlled while at the mercy of others. They feel secure and okay so long as they are in control of their circumstances. They are constantly aiming to move away from external limitations and toward selfsufficiency and power.

Type 9 – The fear of loss and separation from others.

Type 9s strive to maintain peace and harmony both internally and externally. Their pervasive, underlying fear is that they will become disconnected from others and out of sync with the world around them. They feel secure and okay as long as they are living in harmony with the people and world around them. They are constantly moving away from conflict and pain and toward peace, stability and harmony.

Note about basic fears: Though many of us possess more than one basic fear, you must evaluate your Enneagram type by identifying the fear that stands out as the most intense or horrifying to you – the one that perhaps elicits a physiological response when you encounter it and that you feel a drastic gut impulse to avoid. This will be a fear that you have experienced pervasively in your life, across a wide range of situations.

Once you have determined your dominant type, you can then move on to identifying your wing.

I'm Confused about My Wing

Your Enneagram 'wing' is the type that appears either above or below your dominant type numerically. The traits of the 'wing' complement the ones of your dominant type.

Your wing is always the number that either precedes or succeeds the number of your main type – it is not necessarily your second-highest test score. So, if you are a type 7, your wing must be either 6 or 8 – even if the type on which you scored second highest was 4.

The reasons you may have scored second highest on a type that is not your wing is because that number is likely a part of your tritype.

What Are Tritypes?

The Enneagram is divided into three 'triads' or three groups of three personality types.

The 'Feeling Triad' or the 'Heart Triad' is composed of types two, three, and four. We all use one of these three types as our main mode of establishing our self-image. All of the types in the heart triad are motivated by (avoiding their) underlying feelings of shame.

The 'Thinking Triad' or the 'Head Triad' is composed of types five, six, and seven. We all use one of these three types as our main mode of achieving security and managing anxiety. All of the types in the head triad are motivated by (avoiding their) underlying feelings of fear.

The 'Instinctive Triad' or the 'Body Triad' is composed of types eight, nine and one. We all use one of these three types as our main mode of establishing boundaries between the external world and ourselves. All types in the body triad are motivated by (avoiding their) underlying feelings of anger and rage.

Your tritype is composed of your dominant heart type, your dominant head type, and your dominant body type, in order of your preference for using each.

For example: If you use type 2 to govern your heart, type 6 to govern your head and type 9 to govern your body, your tritype would include each of those numbers, in the order of your preference. If you like to predominantly use your head type, then your heart type, then your body type, your tritype would be 6-2-9. Your dominant personality type is always the first number in your tritype. Your wing may or may not be a part of your tritype.

FREE PERSONALITY TESTS - WHAT CAN THEY TEACH YOU?

There are many free personality tests available on the internet. Which ones are worth taking and what can they teach you about yourself? This depends on what you are looking for, of course. Some people just love to take tests and quizzes of all kinds. If you're a member of a social site like Facebook you probably see all kinds of quizzes being added daily. Some of these are fun to take and share with your friends, but they are not likely to be very insightful about your personality or potential.

The purpose of more serious personality tests is to help you find out what your skills, aptitudes, and tendencies are. This can help you plan a new career, decide on a course of study in college, university or technical school or even help you decide what kind of people you should date. The point is - these tests, if they are well constructed, can tell you specific things about yourself that you may not have realized before. More often than not you will say to yourself, "that's right - that's really me!" after taking a test. In other words, you probably knew the information at some level, but never consciously used it or you didn't think it was that important.

A good example of a well-respected personality test is the MyersBriggs typology test (also called MBTI). This test is based on the work of Swiss psychologist Carl Jung. This test divides people into 16 types. I won't describe each one in detail here but to clarify, I'll briefly mention the criteria it uses.

To find out where you fit on the MBTI, you answer many questions, but these are really aspects of four basic questions. First, you find out if you are more introverted or extroverted; this means, basically, if you are more oriented toward the inner or outer. Secondly, you decide if you are more sensing or intuitive - that is, whether you mainly use your senses to see (hear, taste, etc.) the world or if you use your mind or intuition more. Thirdly, it asks if you are more of a thinking or feeling kind of person. That is, do you react more intellectually or emotionally to the world?

Finally, are you more judging or perceiving? This has to do with whether you are someone who plans things out in advance or if you are more spontaneous.

This is a very simplified description, of course. When you answer all of the questions in the test, you have a better idea of how to accurately find out where you stand on these four basic points. Then, you find out what "type" you are. This test is used quite commonly by corporations and other institutions to decide how suitable someone might be for a job. It's also very useful to help you get an idea of what kind of career might suit you, or what kind of people you'd be most comfortable with.

Another popular and well respected personality test is the Enneagram, which was first introduced by the spiritual teacher George Gurdjieff. The Enneagram divides people into nine basic types and it is really a whole school of psychology in itself. There are some good books on the Enneagram, as well as some free tests you can take online to find out which type you are.

WHAT ARE THE ENNEAGRAM WINGS

How can all people be categorized into just nine types? It sounds far too limiting to be reasonable. And while the enneagram is a basic nine point system, there are actually over 60 types and this estimate derives without considering levels of functioning. A number of fine nuances to typing make a difference in how people of different types behave and see the world in a trance.

One of these finer points is the one of "wings". A wing is the subtle influence of the type adjacent to someone's basic Enneagram number. So for example, a two might have either a one wing or a three wing. A two with a one wing will have more concern for propriety while a two with a three wing will tend to be a more hospitable, presentationoriented person.

However, both are helping types, the hallmark of twos.

And this is the way for every type in the Enneagram. Each type will have a potential to be attached to the wing on either side and cause that person's trance to be a bit different from that of people with the other wing.

As people grow older, the other wing will also become more developed but always only one of the wings will be the predominant "flavor" of that person's type.

The beauty of wings is the fine spin that they put on basic types. Let's say that a person has a heart type, such as a four. That person may have either a five wing, which would be a head type and add a more thinking quality to the four personality, or that four type might be coupled with the adjacent three type and would be more into presentations and goal-directed activities on the surface.

For students of the Enneagram, learning to consider wings when looking at one's own or someone else's type and taking into consideration the flavor that a wing adds to someone's personality can be a step forward in understanding the system. For one thing, it makes it clear why people of the same type can seem "different" on the surface. Understanding the main elements of each type and then using them to look carefully at the influences of a wing can bring that person's trance into light. An 8 with a 7 wing will be a bit more mental on top of the feeling component of the 8's and prone to impulsive behavior based on over fear than an 8 with a nine wing who will appear calmer in a domestic situation yet is doubly angerdriven within that triad.

It's important to understand that wings, like types, do not tell the whole story. Sub-types, levels of health, and movement within the Enneagram during times of stress can also affect one's behavior type.

Chapter 5: Points Of Integration And Disintegration And Harmonic Groups

"One of the main tools for entering into the vivid immediacy of quiet mind is "not knowing." Ordinarily, our minds are filled with all kinds of opinions about who we are, what we are doing, what is important and not important, what is right and wrong, and how things ought to turn out. Because our mind is full of opinions and old thoughts, it has no internal space for a fresh impression of the real world around us. We learn nothing new. This also prevents us from really seeing other people - especially the people we love. We imagine that we really know people or even what they are thinking. Many of us know from experience, though, that to experience freshly someone we know can instantly transform our state and theirs. In some cases, this can save a relationship.

Not knowing involves suspending our opinions and letting our curiosity within the realm of quiet mind take the lead", Don Richard Riso, The Wisdom of the Enneagram

One of the fascinating aspects about the dominant type is that it often shifts around the enneagram when they are in different states of mind. They can move to different areas when they are chilled out and relaxing compared to times when they are under stress and anxiety.

These points are often called security or stress points or referred to as integration and disintegration elements.

There are 3 noticeable patterns for all the 9 types in the enneagram. Each of these types share prevalent attributes in their group when they do not get what they would like (or have unfulfilled needs and respond under stress).

Let's Go Deeper

These kinds of aspects are sometimes called security or stress points or known as integration and disintegration points.

Your core personality will shift around yielding different results from an individual depending upon the health level they are under.

Here is a summary of the stress and security elements:

- Type one move to four when under strain and seven when relaxed.

- Type two move to eight when under stress and four when relaxed.

- Type three move to nine when under stress and six when relaxed.

- Type four move to two when under strain and one when relaxed.

- Type five move to seven when under stress and eight when relaxed.

- Type six move to three when under stress and nine when relaxed.

- Type seven move to one when under stress and five when relaxed.

- Type eight move to five when under strain and two when relaxed.

- Type nine move to six when under strain and three when relaxed.

It is said that stress points often create negative outcomes and therefore security points generate only ever beneficial results. This might be true most of the time but it also depends upon the individual's capability to deal with stress and the ability to remain grounded when they are lost in relaxation.

The 3 accordant groups are:

- Positive outlook group

- Competency group

- Emotional authenticity group

The positive outlook group includes the types two, seven and nine. They usually have trouble harmonizing their needs versus the needs of others. They also have difficulty acknowledging the painful process of change, growth and perturbation.

The competency group includes the types one, three and five.

They generally deny their feelings because they believe that they often get in the way of their capability and skills when managing tasks. They also connect to rules in their own unique distinct way.

The emotional authenticity group includes the Enneagram types four, six and eight. They are all psychologically eloquent and vent their feelings to other people constantly. They also count on other people to 'mirror' their emotions. When they have unresolved feelings, they will harbor many grudges and bitterness. However, once they address their feelings and deal with the issue at hand, things typically blow over swiftly and they are more forgiving once these repressed negative feelings are resolved.

Chapter 6: The Enneagram Personality

Type 3 - The Performer

This personality type is also called the Achiever or the Chameleon. This person is driven for success and is determined to achieve their goals no matter what. This person needs to achieve success and to be admired by others so that they feel validated in their worth as individuals. As a result, these people are hard-working, competitive, and highly focused in the pursuit of achieving their goals. These types of people know how to get the job done in the most efficient way possible and always like to celebrate ticking the task off their to-do list.

What Makes the Performer a Great Personality

THE PERFORMER IS SUCCESS-ORIENTED. This personality type is driven to be the best they can be and even likes to motivate others in the same positive way. As a result of this, they are held in high regard by others. The Performer is often the person who is voted the class president or the one that others should aspire to be like. Because of their drive for success, they are often seen as the embodiment of role models so that others can invest in their own self-development.

THE PERFORMER IS HARD-WORKING. Because of the need to achieve success, this personality type places a lot of energy in getting the job done.

THE PERFORMER IS EXTROVERTED AND OUTGOING. Performers are often highly socially competent and extroverted. They are highly charismatic and know how to present themselves to others as self-confident, practical, and driven. They draw energy from crowds and often have that energy that other people find contagious. This results in them being good networkers and often rise very quickly through the ranks because they know how to rub elbows with the best of them.

The Deadly Sins of the Performer

THE PERFORMER IS IMAGE-CONSCIOUS. The Performer loves being the center of attention and loves gaining praise from others. Therefore, they often cultivate the way that they look and act to meet the standard that other persons have placed for them. This person wants to be admired and feels a deep sense of loss when they do not feel that this is the case.

THE PERFORMER NEEDS EXTERNAL VALIDATION. While the Performer is success-oriented, oftentimes their definition of success is defined by someone else such as their family, social sphere, or culture. They hold the values and ideas of others in high regard and feel like if they do not meet that standard that they are nobody. They also crave the positive attention and praise that meeting the standard of achievement gains. As a result of this, the Performer can become alienated because they do not know what they truly want or are not truly in touch with their own feelings and interests.

THE PERFORMER FINDS IT DIFFICULT TO FORM DEEP EMOTIONAL TIES. Performers are often secretly afraid of being labeled losers. As a result, they find intimacy with others difficult and because of the need for validation, they often hide a deep sense of shame for who they truly are. These persons often miss out on developing deeply loving relationships and cultivating personal experiences because they are so laser-focused on the outer world and not on nurturing their inner being and the relationships that they form. The fear manifests itself by them pushing others away so that no one gets close enough to unmask the negative feelings that they harbor. This makes types 3s very difficult people to get to know.

THE PERFORMER IS SELF-DECEPTIVE. Because of the need for external validation, type 3s are often good at self-deception because even when they appear to be happy, they carry a deep sense of meaninglessness. No matter how strong their social strengths, Performers are often secretly afraid of being labeled losers and overcompensate so that no one else finds out about their deep-rooted fears. Because they are such hard workers, Performers often suffer from burn outs because they do not know when to quit.

THE PERFORMER CAN BE UNETHICAL. It is quite common for them to cut corners so that they accomplish their goals in as little time as possible. Even though they are often generous and very likeable people, they can become very ruthless and cold-hearted in the pursuit of excellence and their goals.

How the Performer Relates to Other Personality Types

The Performers vs. Type 1s

Please see Chapter 2: How Reformers Relate to Other Personality Types: Reformers vs. Type 3s.

The Performers vs. Type 2s

Please see Chapter 3: How Helpers Relate to Other Personality Types: Helpers vs. Type 3s.

The Performers vs. Type 4s

These two personality types form a complementary relationship because they play on each other's strengths and compensate for each other's weaknesses. Type 4s can help the Performer access their emotions on a deeper level and help them process their feelings while the Performer can help types 4s handle their emotional reactions with more tact and diplomacy, as well as help ease their self-doubts. Because both of these personality types are both image conscientious they often exude a sense of style and enjoyment for the finer things in life as a couple. Trouble may arise because both of these personality types have self-esteem issues and need attention and validation from external sources. They both harbor questions about their own identity and feel worthless quite easily. This can create a codependency that is unhealthy.

The Performers vs. Type 5s

These two personality types are a frequent combination since type 5s help the Performer gain increased emotional depth, gain expertise in new areas, and become more creative. The Performer helps type 5s get increased self-confidence, better communication skills with others, and better presentation skills. Both of these personality types are focused on their work, are competent and effective. Therefore, they are great at supporting each other while not crowding each other and respecting each other's need for space. As a couple they are well-respected, sharp, and successful. On the flip side of the coin, because of their high competency and focus on work, this can lead to conflict, tension, and elements of competitiveness. Because both of these personality types do not readily speak of their feelings, they can easily grow cold and distant from each other.

The Performers vs. Type 6s

The pairing of these two personality types does not occur often, even though they work very well as a team. Performers bring a hard-working ethic, a desire for communication, ease of connection with other people, and energy to the relationship. Type 6s introduce support and practical sense to the union. As long as they remain grounded, these two personality types can form a successful and enduring union. Unfortunately these two personality types can also bring out the worst in each other because they have similar negative qualities. They are both very competitive, easily fall into workaholism, look for external sources of validation, and want to be socially accepted. This can give rise to dishonesty, evasiveness, and covert measures to meet their personal needs, which can quickly deteriorate their relationship.

The Performers vs. Type 7s

The pairing of these two personality types are complementary as they are both selfless, high energy, capable in social situations, and outgoing. They bring optimism and future-orientation to the relationship. Even though Performers work alone more readily than type 7s, they are both excellent communicators, persuasive, articulate, and stimulated by the interactions with other people. As a pair, they are generous and fun to be around. Unfortunately, the pair can also be extremely volatile because they are both such high energy types. They also feel a need to project perfection as a couple, which can put a strain on their connection and interaction with each other.

The Performers vs. Type 8s

The pairing of these two personality types can form quite the power couple because they are both assertive and go after the things that they want in life. They often form a pair because they cannot help but notice each other because both shine so brightly as a personality. Even though they are both decisive and strong characters, they tend not to be competitive with each other even though they both have a competitive nature with other people. Their weakness lies in the fact that they both tend to be workaholics and put themselves under a lot of stress in order to achieve their goals. Because they are so focused on achieving their goals, they might not support each other as needed. Type 8s also tend to be controlling, suspicious, and distrusting of others. They may need the Performer to do things that proves his or her loyalty and this results in type 3s feeling used and belittled. This leads to the deterioration of the relationship.

The Performers vs. Type 9s

The pairing of these two personality types is fairly common. Type 9s provide support, encouragement, and pride in the Performer's achievements. Performers help type 9s find value in themselves, develop higher levels of self-respect, and seek investment in their own self-development. The pairing of these two personality types work so well because they are so supporting and accepting of each other. The potential conflict that can arise in this type of relationship is the fact that neither wants to bring up any potential conflicts that they have. This means that problems may fester and introduce fragility into the relationship.

How the Performer Can Improve His or Her Life

The Performer needs to learn to slow down and to form genuine connections with other people as well as get to the heart of his or her true desires. While the Performer does not need to ditch being goal-oriented, this person does need to learn to prioritize goals that benefit them holistically rather than just to gain approval from others. Chakra meditations that are useful to this personality type are the sacral chakra meditation, which is useful in allowing this person to become more in-tune with their feelings, and a heart chakra meditation, which allows for developing compassion and sensitivity internally and externally.

Acupressure application also works for this person. The points that need to be stimulated include:

●SI-19. Stimulating this acupressure point allows a person to be more in tune with their heart's desires as well as the hearts of other people. The point is located near the ear just before the small projection in front of the opening of the ear canal.

●SP-6. As mentioned before, stimulating this acupressure point, which is found on the inside of the lower leg above the ankle, aids in relaxation and a reduction in irritability.

●TB-17. Stimulating this acupressure point helps a person become less sensitive to what other people think about them. It is located behind the ear lobe at the bottom of the ear.

Other ways in which the Performer can improve his or her life include:

●Being honest with his or herself and others about their feelings and needs to project authenticity.

●Resisting the temptation to impress others.

●Resisting performing actions just to be accepted by others. This allows for the discovery of their own core values.

●Learning to develop deeper connections in their relationships. This can be as simple as taking time to have one-on-one conversation with an individual.

●Scheduling breaks in the pursuit of their goals so that they can recharge their battery and improve their outlook on life.

●Pursuing activities that allow for personal advancement rather than just bringing social awareness to themselves.

●Pursuing different types of hobbies so that they can find out what truly resonates with them.

●Resisting the urge to cut corners and remain ethical while pursuing their goals.

Chapter 7: The 9 Enneagram Personality Types

1 THE REFORMER

The Rational, Idealistic Type: Principled, Purposeful, Self-Controlled, and Perfectionistic

2 THE HELPER

The Caring, Interpersonal Type: Demonstrative, Generous, People-Pleasing, and Possessive

3 THE ACHIEVER

The Success-Oriented, Pragmatic Type: Adaptive, Excelling, Driven, and Image-Conscious

4 THE INDIVIDUALIST

The Sensitive, Withdrawn Type: Expressive, Dramatic, Self-Absorbed, and Temperamental

5 THE INVESTIGATOR

The Intense, Cerebral Type: Perceptive, Innovative, Secretive, and Isolated

6 THE LOYALIST

The Committed, Security-Oriented Type: Engaging, Responsible, Anxious, and Suspicious

7 THE ENTHUSIAST

The Busy, Fun-Loving Type: Spontaneous, Versatile, Distractible, and Scattered

8 THE CHALLENGER

The Powerful, Dominating Type: Self-Confident, Decisive, Willful, and Confrontational

9 THE PEACEMAKER

The Easygoing, Self-Effacing Type: Receptive, Reassuring, Agreeable, and Complacent

Characterizing Characteristics of the Enneagram Type 9

Investigate THE 9 ENNEAGRAM TYPES

The Enneagram alludes to the nine distinct sorts or styles, with each speaking to a perspective and paradigm that resounds with the manner in which individuals think, feel and act in connection to the world, others and themselves. It is considerably more than a character profile that offers knowledge into center character characteristics, as it dives further into the center inspirations, safeguard instruments and fears that regularly lie in the oblivious layers of our character structure. Your Enneagram center sort resembles a command post from which we understand individuation, mix and improvement. Different words used to depict 'type' incorporate reverberation, distinguishing proof, focal point, viewpoint or style.

It is critical to remember that diverse Enneagram styles may show comparative conduct. The Enneagram styles are not founded on conduct alone, and outward conduct can be misdirecting while investigating the Enneagram. To recognize styles, it is critical to get to inspiration – to investigate why an individual decides to act with a particular goal in mind and why acting in that way is esteemed by that person.

Enneagram 9 Strengths

Each character paradigm has qualities and vulnerable sides, and these are regularly enhanced in proficient settings where we frequently experience a various gathering of individuals with tremendously various foundations and worth frameworks.

Enneagram 9 Strengths

Qualities that are ordinarily connected with the Enneagram 9 character incorporate:

Capacity to see different points of view

Keeping quiet and versatile

Supporting and consoling everyone around them

Interceding strife between others

Being liberal and suspending judgment

Chapter 8: Enneagram, You And Us

Like an onion, let us add another layer that will assist in decrypting relationships.

We have a better chance at becoming more focused and considerate when we are

mindful of our intellectual and behavioral selves. We then have a say in how we

choose to act. The Enneagram gives us a tool to identify strengths and eliminate

weaknesses...or at least bury them a bit. Consider then; we can learn about others.

It is important to mention that the key to improving relationships whether they are

friendly, romantic or professional, all parties involved need to be open to talking

about their needs and listening to others'. When we own our experiences,

understand and empathize with those around us. Researchers all over the world have tried to untangle differences in demographics, values, gender roles and status

to find an aha moment that will explain why some relationships work and others

fail. Those efforts are inconsistent and full of mixed outcomes.

So far, we have only touched the surface on the types of application you can use the

knowledge gained from the Enneagram. There is increasing information specific

to how relationships can be improved by using the ages-old concept of the

Enneagram in all areas of our lives.

A beautiful asset of the Enneagram is that it does not tell us which person should

be drawn to another by numbers. Instead, it allows for the opportunity of various

types to be attracted to one another in a healthy stage and build a balanced

collection of positive traits. This is because an individual is no longer held captive by their innate or reactive impulses but strengthened by awareness and knowledge

of more acceptable behaviors and responses.

We can set goals and visualize our changes by achieving them. A modern

mnemonic makes goal-setting easier and tangible:

☐S – Specific

☐M – Measurable

☐A – Attainable

☐R – Realistic

☐T – Timely

Using the information you learned about yourself through Enneagram tests and

applying it to the above steps to setting your goals is universal. It is a great way to

enhance yourself, build on relationships, and facilitate success in school or at work.

The Enneagram has a lot of research predominantly supporting its spiritual and intimate applications. However, there is a new trend that supports how this

process can be used in business to find solutions and improve business for both

employees and managers.

Chapter 9: Know Your Enneagram Type:

Personality Test

By reading our introduction you are probably raring to find out which your personality type is, and from there you can jump to the page which describes you.

Well, before you come to that conclusion, you need to realise that we all have a basic personality type, but learning about all nine is the best way to truly understand yourself, because everyone has a tiny facet of the other types in them too.

First things first however, how do you find out your core type?

Brutal honesty is the way forward!

Finding out your core personality type in truth is not a short process and it is something which takes time and thought. There are countless Enneagram tests online which will help you gain some insight, and the RHETI (Riso-Hudson Enneagram Type Indicator) is the most commonly used. This particular test has been scientifically validated, and is thought to be around 80% accurate in most cases. On top of this, another credible source is the TAS Questionnaire in The Wisdom of Enneagram. Again, this is scientifically validated, and offers the same high level of accuracy.

There are many shorter online personality tests you can take, if you want to simply start thinking about what type of personality you are, before giving in to self-reflection to truly arrive at the most accurate result for you.

•Think carefully, think about how you react, how you feel, and how you behave on a daily basis

●Be totally and brutally honest, even ask a close friend or family member to list your attributes and behavior patterns if that helps

●Take an online personality test and assess the results – do you agree with them?

●Use a scientifically validated test, such as the TAS Questionnaire, or the RHETI, which we mentioned above

●Think a little more – do you agree with the results? It's important to realise that you might be surprised, so don't discount the results because you simply don't think you display a certain characteristic; you might have it without realizing! Again, ask a close friend or family member for advice

●Once you have gone through this process you should finally come up with a type which reflects you.

We are rarely purely one type

Throughout your decision journey, it's important to note that we are very rarely one type only; we are complicated beings, and therefore we display characteristics of various types – however with that in mind, there should be one type which comes up time and time again, and that is your core personality type.

Whilst we are all born with one particular main type within us, it's likely that this doesn't really show itself too much until the teenage years appear which we all know is a time of experiment and self-discovery in itself. During the 20s, the main personality type will show itself more so, and this is when Enneagram becomes much easier to pinpoint.

Once you realise which personality type you truly are, the journey certainly does not end there

Quite frankly, the whole palava is only just beginning!

The whole point of Enneagram is to use your personality type results to help you understand your inner being in a much more detailed way. Once you figure out which is your main personality type, this is just step one on your journey to self-discovery, self-development, and self-enlightenment.

You can use your results to pinpoint the negative parts of your personality and improve upon them; however it's also worthwhile knowing that everyone has their faults, so Enneagram is never going to make you a 100% perfect person. On top of this, understanding your strengths by pinpointing your personality type can allow you to develop them further, and use them for good, rather than negative causes.

What are Levels of Development?

If you have read anything about Enneagram before, you might have heard of Levels of Development, and you might be wondering what this is all about.

Once you pinpoint your core personality type, you can begin your journey into developing your understanding, using the results to develop as a person. Levels of Development therefore describe how an individual's personality type shifts and changes as they become more familiar with it, and as they develop more a person overall.

Over time, everyone heads upwards and downwards within the line level of their particular personality type, and this changes especially as an individual becomes more au fait with their type, and as a result, their true inner being.

Different personality types

In our coming chapters we will discuss each of the nine personality types in detail. Whilst it is important to truly explore the type you are, e.g. if you are identified as a type four, you should read and re-read that particular chapter; you should also read the others, because as we have discussed, everyone has facets of every type of personality to some degree or another, and to truly understand yourself as a person, and your inner and higher being, you need to see every single facet of it.

Of course, you could also argue that understanding all nine personality types can help you in your social life too, as understanding other people is key to having healthy, functioning relationships, in your personal, work, and social lives.

Chapter 10: Your Evolving, Revolving,

Dissolving Self

You may know yourself pretty well by now and there may be some aspects of your personality that you admit and adore and live your life by.

Life is lived in comparison with our fellow Beings and the quickest way to knowing yourself well is by how you judge how others seem to be behaving. When you describe yourself as 'I'm the kind of person who....' or 'I would NEVER do a thing like that!' then you are recognising the qualities of your essential self – OR the idealistic version of yourself.

Your Evolving Self

Now, when life is hunky dory and you are feeling on top of the world, chances are you are in a state of Evolving. Some say this is the true meaning of life; to keep moving forward, despite setbacks, to forge ahead even when the world seems against you. Evolving can be very pleasant, or it can be hell on earth though evolving is the true aim of the Universe, of which you are part.

You will have your number type, though also the number that you evolve to - evolving to the very BEST of that number.

Your Revolving Self

This is where you live most of the time, often going around and around in circles, thinking thoughts you thought yesterday and getting the same reactions you would expect from your relationship to money, the environment, your own body and other people – unless you are far more enlightened than most and committed to improving yourself and your condition the majority of the time.

Your Dissolving Self

When the stresses and strains of life become too much to bear, we retreat into negative states. Those negative states are familiar and well worn and if particular patterns keep repeating in your life then you know this cycle all too well.

Happily, the Enneagram provides you with a map. This enables you to recognise your numbered personality 'type' and typically those behaviours thoughts and feelings you retreat to when anxious, upset, angry or apathetic, for example.

You will have the number given that you dissolve to - dissolving to the very WORST of that number.

Unwanted Behaviour

We can no more easily halt our unwanted behaviour patterns any more than we can prevent our hand being pulled spontaneously from something hot, or tickly, or sharp. Berating an unwanted behaviour is one small step away from berating ourselves.

We are not our Behaviours

In the same way as we would instinctively pull that hand away from the hot flame or sharp pin, so we instinctively react to circumstance when under undue stress.

Everyone is the same? Know Thyself

We may all share certain characteristics, though we all have our differing personalities and as we grow older and begin to accept our talents and flaws, these traits become more apparent.

It's Just Me!

This is what your Negative Ego (which does not want you to know that everything is indeed ONE and that hating your brother is hating yourself, ultimately) would have you believe.

It wants you to think that you are special, you are alone, you are the only one and no one has or is suffering or has had it as hard as you have.

You are a Number!

Nooooooo! 'I am not a number, I am a free man', comes the cry. There was a time, like most of my life, when I would have argued against this. I hated being categorised and yet it is so helpful when you do place yourself on this map. When you recognise the energies at work upon you and how to rise above them, or chose to accept them and wallow in the understanding(!) is a huge relief.

Enlightenment

It's like a light goes on; the penny drops. I found it easier to place myself on the map when I admitted my dissolving state; how I behave when overwhelmed with stress.

Then I had lots of reflections back at me when mentioning my findings to others, who, by the way, can serve as a mirror of ourselves.

Comments such as, 'Oh yes! You do that ALL the time and it drives me crazy', gives you the realisation that perhaps you are on the right lines.

'Absolutely not! You might like to think that, BUT what you really do when something doesn't go your way is....', means you may have to revisit the map!

Finding Direction

This Kitching Whittaker Enneagram is far more than mere 'personality typing' as it gives you a clear direction in how to progress your personality into a positive direction, using your drives and instincts and propelling yourself into that evolving desired state.

At the very least you can go lick your wounds in the corner and realise that you know yourself far better than you used to and that if the map can be right about this awful stuff you feel right now, then perhaps it is worth some time and interest to explore.

What a Coincidence! We happen to be on the very same planet at the very same time!

Of course you are not alone. Even if you wanted to be, sooner or later you have to interact with others, when you can then judge them for being nice and helpful or bloody minded and obstructive. This again, will point you to your number type and be helpful in empathising with others and/or dissociating more from them if you wish!

Mood Swings

As we are all various personality types, 9 in total, being affected by circumstance and fluctuating energies constantly, it is a wonder that any of us get along with each other at all! Yet we do. In fact, there are certain individuals we spend a whole lifetime with, often understanding and making allowances for their varying moods and tantrums far more than we will ever tolerate of ourselves.

Chapter 11: Ten Detailed Steps To

Transform Your Life

Now that you have gained a precious understanding about yourself and your personality type, it's time to put it to good use. You will need a strategy to transform your life and finally achieve your ultimate goals. Here is a detailed list of steps you should follow to make sure you accomplish your goals.

Be willing to take this journey

Willingness to change seems like an obvious step, but many of us forget about getting ourselves mentally prepared beforehand. Self-discovery can be intense, so you must be willing and ready to dig deep, sometimes even finding and accepting some information about yourself that you dislike because you know it is for a greater purpose.

Establishing your goals

Knowing what you want and why you are going through this personal transformation is also an important step. Your journey might change slightly along the way, so you should make sure that the goals you establish for yourself are realistic and attainable. For example, I wanted to become a more independent and secure person, and in the back of my mind while I was discovering my personality type and my traits, I always kept that ultimate goal in sight.

Learning about your personality type

Find out what your personality type is and understand it. By taking one of the personality tests discussed earlier, you will be better able to understand your personality traits. It's important to read about your personality type and relate it to how you have lived your life so far. You might also see detect some of the other personality types characteristics in you, and that's very common. You can't be purely a "Challenger" or a 100 percent "Loyalist." The enneagram will be very helpful to actually comprehend what personality strengths and weaknesses you display and build from there.

Making the changes

Although it might not be a simple process, by analyzing your personality type, you will understand where you need to improve, or change some of your behaviors or thought processes. Introvert, extrovert, fearless or cautious, you will adjust the characteristic you want to change badly enough by taking them one day at a time.

Perhaps you really need to be in a different relationship, to shine more, or you simply need to better understand the personality of other people in order to communicate and get along better. What is absolutely necessary to your success is also to embrace these changes that you are putting in place. If you are resistant, you are the only one standing in your way to personal transformation.

Learning from your trials

Because you will be trying to change something that is probably very heavily anchored in you, such as your inability to trust or your naiveté, expect that it will be a process filled with trials. When you trip, don't beat yourself up, but instead be happy that the experience provides you with a learning opportunity. If you have always been the one to think about others and constantly forget about yourself, you will have a hard time changing that trait for good. You may say yes when you really mean no, and that's totally okay. However, you will remember next time how you felt about giving in and forgetting to claim your ground, and you will simply remedy the situation the next time. You will learn to say no and be okay with it.

Adopting the right attitude

Positivity is the key, and you always need to believe in what you are implementing, because if not, then who will? There are many ways to achieve a positive attitude, and meditation is one means to help you break away and focus your thoughts on what you are trying to accomplish. By refocusing and having a clear mind, you can do whatever you are trying to do much more efficiently. Also, the repetition of positive affirmations can truly be powerful when you are undergoing any change. For instance, on your way to work or to a meeting, repeat to yourself how much power or courage you have, if you are currently trying to work on your courage.

Reevaluating your goals/dreams

Recommit. Because you have identified what it is about your personality that you dislike or would like to be different, you will most likely need to reorient your life in many sectors as well. So sit down and write down your new goals and evaluate them for the short and long term. For example, maybe you know you have that leader skill within you but in the past, you were always too afraid of failure. Now that you have practice to rebalance your personality traits, you can definitely start looking into starting your own business. So go for it!

Get the needed support

Do not be afraid to involve other people in your life-changing process. For example, if you are in a stable relationship, your new goals will certainly impact your spouse, so get him or her up to speed. They can be your allies, and they should be. Your relationship should be improving both of your lives. You can also recruit help from others in your professional or even spiritual life. Don't be shy about explaining to your children what you are trying to accomplish, as they can learn valuable life lessons and also be your biggest supporter, as you are trying to adjust certain behaviors and responses to others. Work on carefully surrounding yourself with the right people to succeed in your life-changing quest.

Accepting yourself fully

Finally, at the end of this exercise or journey, you will learn the most valuable lesson of all: love and acceptance of yourself. By being conscious of whom you are and simply changing your actions depending on the situations and circumstances, that's a plus. Your environment could also be what needs to be adapted or changed, so look into this possibility as well.

Rewarding yourself

It's essential to recognize and celebrate your successes. So when you have reached one of your goals or able to progress in your personal transformation, pat yourself on the back. It will help you keep going and often make you evaluate what has worked, so you can repeat it next time.

Chapter 12: Type Three Personality

Type Three (performer and achiever) - As a performer, they want to be productive in whatever they lay their hands on. As an achiever, they have an insatiable desire to succeed in all their endeavors. They are driven by the need to excel and get ahead of their peers and colleagues. Results mean everything to them; they talk in facts and figures rather than babble around with mere rhetoric.

The characteristics of Type Threes are as follows -

● Type Three personality trait individuals long for admiration from others. This rationalizes their desire to succeed in whatever they do. Receiving praise for their efforts gives them a sense of pride and this could lead to an inflated ego. They are self-motivated and want to get things done. As subordinates or members of a team, they need not be coerced to perform their tasks especially, when such tasks are rewarded with individual glory.

● Type Three's love to publicize and promote themselves to show off their achievements. Type Threes would not allow others to take or even share in their glory. They don't just want to produce results, they also want to be seen to do so. On the negative side, they want to distance themselves from things that are not producing desirable results. If this plays out in a team, they would still want to single themselves out as exceptional and result-oriented.

● Type Three's place a premium importance on their physical appearance and want to look really good to members of both sexes. When it comes to looking good, they are not averse to spending a sizeable portion of their income on good fashion. A person's physical appearance adds to or diminishes his or her confidence and Type Threes place a great deal on emphasis on this fact. If they feel their looks are not okay, they would rather not go out on a date or to some other public place.

● Type Three's enjoy being the figurehead or a symbolic individual within their groups or units. If it were possible for them to nominate themselves for a leadership role like a team leader, they would do it without hesitation. This is usually the case even when they are not deserving of such a role. They dislike hiding in the shadows for long, be it on a campus or office or church. Whether by election or selection, they want to occupy leadership positions that can give them opportunities for growth and advancement.

● Type Three's are more likely to pursue success and achievement at the expense of the core values they should protect. This may bring out the worst in them and cause them to engage in horrible acts of all kinds. Ethical conduct may mean little or nothing to them on their way to realizing their personal aspirations. They find themselves at the two extremes of morality and this means they can either morally conduct themselves or are savages in their pursuit of personal and work goals.

• Being part of the emotional or feeling group, Type Threes like to interact with people who can help them achieve their set goals. This does not imply that Type Three personalities are very social but they can become social with a specific objective in mind. Nevertheless, they have a good ability to shield their feelings from others if that will enable them to hit a target. They would prefer to handle emotional or personal issues alone rather than share it with others.

• Type Threes do not shy away from rivalry with others be it in school, at work, in the family or any kind of setting at all. They can be so obsessed with being better than others that they may sacrifice relationships no matter how valuable such people are to them. A Type Three believes that cut-throat competition is an inevitable part of life and in their opinion, we are all competing in a race against each other. If they fight and run away, they would definitely be back to fight another day. It has little to do with their physical size or mental ability but the amount of fight in them which is usually at a high level.

• Type Threes enjoy a lot of physical activity especially those taking place outdoors. If they have a choice between indoor and outdoor activities, they would choose the later and they are likely to be seen engaging in physical activities like gardening or swimming as long as their bodies can cope. Only issues like aging, disability or illness can stop Type Threes from taking part in recreation. Being a natural competitor, they are willing to put huge demands on their physical bodies in order to excel in sports and recreational activities.

Below is the list of renowned 'Type three' personalities in human history -

• BILL CLINTON - The 42nd President of the United States who left office with a very high end-of-office approval rating. He was also the former attorney general and governor of the state of Arkansas. Despite the fact that his image was badly damaged by a sex scandal in the White House, he still managed to rebuild his reputation and had the highest end-of-office approval rating of any United States president since World War II. His Type Three nature also manifested when he successfully secured the release of two American journalists imprisoned by North Korea.

- MUHAMMAD ALI - An American professional boxer, activist and philanthropist who is widely regarded as one of the most significant and celebrated sports figures of the 20th century. He has been ranked as the leading heavyweight boxer of all time and some of his boxing records were unmatched for more than three decades after his retirement. Being a Type Three, Muhammad Ali is no doubt a smooth-talking 'marketer.' At a time when most fighters let their managers do the talking, he thrived in and indeed craved the spotlight, where he was often provocative and outlandish. He was known for trash-talking and often free-styled with popular rhymes as a means of intimidating his opponents.

- ARNOLD SCHWARZENEGGER - An Austrian-American actor and politician who served two terms as the governor of California. He is also considered as one of the greatest bodybuilders of all time as well as the sport's most charismatic ambassador. He is also an author, businessman, activist, and philanthropist. He has always been a fierce competitor from his youth and this trait saw him switch careers regardless of the hurdles in his way. He always wanted to be the very best in whatever he did, be it bodybuilding or acting or business or politics.

- OPRAH WINFREY - An American talk show host, actress, and philanthropist. She is best known for her self-named television show which is the highest rated television programme of its kind in history and was nationally syndicated for over two decades. She is reputed as the richest African American of the 20th century,

North America's first black multi-billionaire and sometimes the most influential woman in the world. Right from an early age, she showed her oratory abilities and this enabled her to access the broadcasting industry as a teenager. The Type Three personality in her was reflected in overcoming adversity to become a benefactor to others.

- MICHAEL JORDAN - An American former professional basketball player who is widely regarded as the greatest basketball player of all time. He was one of the most effectively marketed athletes of his generation and played a vital role in popularising American basketball around the world. He is also the first billionaire player in the history of American basketball. In high school, he was dropped from the senior basketball team because of his height and this made him prove his mettle in the junior team which earned him a spot on the senior team after adding a few inches. His motivation to succeed also saw him temporarily leaving basketball to become a baseball player. He was known throughout his career to be a strong clutch performer; his competitiveness was visible in his prolific trash-talk and well-known work ethic.

• BENJAMIN NETANYAHU - An Israeli politician serving as the current Prime Minister of Israel and has been elected to occupy that position a fourth time. At the expiration of his current term, he will become the longest-serving Israeli prime minister in history. At the Massachusetts Institute of Technology, he completed a four-year masters programme in two and a half years despite taking a break to fight in the Yom Kippur War while simultaneously completing a thesis in a graduate course at Harvard. This demonstrates his workaholic and status-seeker attributes that are characteristic of Type Threes. Netanyahu is also excellent at networking with others and for many years has maintained personal relationships with notable personalities like former Italian Prime Minister Silvio Berlusconi, Hungarian Prime Minister Viktor Orban, United States President

Donald Trump and former Presidential Candidate Mitt Romney.

- VINCE LOMBARDI - An American football player, coach and executive in the National Football League (NFL). After his death, the NFL Super Bowl was named after him and he was also included in the Pro Football Hall of Fame. He is considered by many to be the greatest coach in American football history and also recognised as one of the greatest coaches and leaders in the history of any American sport. When he took over the Green Bay Packers in 1959, the performance of the team was the worst in its history and this demoralised the players, shareholders and indeed the entire Green Bay community. He then introduced tough training programmes and demanded extra effort and dedication from his players. There were noticeable improvement almost immediately and in his second year, the team won the NFL Western Conference for the first time in decades.

- MICHAEL DELL - An American businessman, author, and philanthropist who is the founder and current CEO of Dell Technologies, one of the largest technology infrastructure companies. He is also one of the top 50 richest people in the world. He started his first business as a teenager and he used his company's first financial statement to convince his parents of his decision to drop out of college. The drive to compete and succeed in the computer market saw him winning bids ahead of brick-and-mortar stores even though he was operating from his dormitory.

The typical roles played by Type Threes include -

- THE STATUS SEEKER - a Type Three is willing to give all in the pursuit of image-enhancing status. They want to be the very best version of whatever they do and stand out wherever they find themselves. Where others are satisfied with a first degree, they would not rest until they have gotten a doctorate degree. If others put in four hours of practice, they want to invest half their day in same.

● THE IMAGE BUILDER - They seek to constantly project a good image about themselves to the outside world and are very conscious about how they are perceived by others. Even when this image does not conform to reality, they still want to be seen in a positive light by those that matter.

● THE CON ARTIST - this is not a good side of them as they have an instinctive ability to gain the trust of others and use that confidence as a means of swindling or cheating others. They are masters of the art and science of deception especially when such deception will propel them towards their goals. They want to win by any means possible.

● THE HERO/HEROINE - being the star in any group endeavour or plans means a lot to them. They want to be regarded as the individual who saved the day and thereafter recognized as such. They won't mind receiving all the praise even when the results are not entirely dependent on their efforts.

- THE SPIN DOCTOR - They are also adept at laundering the image of other people especially their superiors or bosses who act in their favor. They can paint a very beautiful and appealing picture about the most unpleasant people, as long as such people patronize or favor them.

- THE MARKETER - Type Three personalities is a smooth-talking flatterer that can persuade just about anyone to buy the snake oil on offer; they can literally sell ice to inhabitants of the Arctic. This is a positive attribute if they have a good or useful product to sell. If not, they could make people buy into stuff they would later regret.

- THE NETWORKER - They love to connect with people wherever they go, especially those from whom meaningful value can be derived. They are not shy about approaching and meeting with anyone who can help them ascend to the next level in their careers and businesses.

● THE COMPETITOR - They anticipate competition and would not back down when it does show up. Getting involved in a rivalry with others gives them an opportunity to stretch their abilities and resources. Even a huge loss or defeat would not deter them from rivalries in the future regardless of apparent gains.

● THE FASHION FREAK - Type Threes love to match colors, wear outfits that are in vogue and make use of accessories that compliment their wears. They pay attention to the smallest of details, things that most people would not probably notice. People may not be overly concerned if a Type Three woman exhibits this particular trait but when a man does, he could be referred to as a dandy.

● THE WORKAHOLIC - Finding a favorable work-life balance means little or nothing to a Type Three. They want to go all out to achieve set targets regardless of what their bodies or doctors say. If this trait is highly dominant in an individual, his or her domestic or family life may suffer undesirable consequences.

A typical Three is an exuberant self-confident person who is easy to notice wherever he or she goes. This confidence is exemplified in their speech, physical appearance or dressing, demeanor and countenance. Whether you like Type Threes or not, at least one of the things mentioned will definitely get your attention. Sometimes, they may put up a bold face to hide certain feelings beneath their lovely apparel. You would not have to force them to smile as such things come naturally to them. They place me-I-myself above everything else, not minding the consequences. On a positive side, they can be self-motivated, responsible, energetic, confident and efficient. On a negative side, they can be controlling, narcissistic, deceptive, self-absorbed, impatient and pretentious.

Chapter 15: Type Four– The Individualist

Fours are sensitive and introspective. They can be dramatic and expressive about the situations happening in their life. They can also be self-absorbed and temperamental.

Fours are very self-aware which can also make them feel self-conscious of their faults. They dwell on the characteristics that make them defective and what they can do to create an identity separate from those around them. They typically have a negative self-image and low self-esteem.

While they tend to be emotionally honest and personal, their self-consciousness can also make them more reserved. They may withdraw from others when they become vulnerable and feel defective.

They want to be extraordinary and have great disdain for living ordinary lifestyles. This causes them to have problems with their self-worth when melancholy and self-indulgence creep in, developing a sense of self-pity.

On a positive note, Fours are highly creative and inspired. They use their creativity to transform experiences. They are able to use inspiration to renew their spirits.

Fours true desire is to find their identity and discover every aspect of their personality. Fours typically feel as if they are lacking, but they usually can't pinpoint exactly what they feel they lack in. Their biggest fear is not being able to leave behind a significant legacy for others to remember them by.

They want to be seen as an individualist that can stand out in a crowd. In a relationship, they desire someone who will appreciate the identity they have created. Fours need someone who sees them as unique and appreciates their uniqueness even more than they do.

Healthy Fours can own up to their feelings and appreciate the little things that make them unique. They are not ashamed of their setbacks and weaknesses. They would rather embrace their true identity even if they don't like what they see.

Lower level Fours may create a "Fantasy Self-Image" of who they want to be. In their mind, they may embellish their skills and abilities. However, when asked to perform these special skills, they become embarrassed because the truth doesn't match their fantasy.

The harshness they put on themselves does allow them to endure painful experiences better than other types. Fours may hang on their negativities until it starves them of happiness. They won't recognize their treasures until they stop putting themselves down and start living up to positive affirmations.

Fours with a Three-Wing are seen as "The Aristocrat," while Fours with a Five-wing are seen as "The Bohemian."

Stress Point

When Type Fours are stressed, they may exhibit negative or unhealthy levels of development typically seen in Type Two personalities.

These unhealthy traits include:

People-pleaser

Intrusive

Presumptuous

Manipulative

Domineering

Victimized

Security Point

During times of growth Type Fours may exhibit positive or healthy levels of development typically seen in Type One personalities.

These healthy traits include:

Wise

Discerning

Conscientious

Principled

Responsible

Ethical

Levels of Development

Healthy:

Level 1

Creative

Fours express themselves and their perceived universe through art. They transform their situations into valuable learning experiences.

Level 2

Introspective

They are aware of their personal feeling and attributes. They can be sensitive to themselves. They are tactful, gentle, and compassionate toward others.

Level 3

Individualistic

They are able to reveal their emotions honestly. They have an ironic view on life. They can be both serious and funny. They may be emotionally strong but also vulnerable.

Average:

Level 4

Imaginative

They use their fantasies to beautify their life.

Level 5

Hypersensitive

They may become too in touch with feelings. They take everything personally. They may become introverted and self-conscious.

Level 6

Self-pity

They are impractical in their view of their lifestyle. They feel they are exempt from living like an "ordinary" person. They envy those with more exciting lifestyle, becoming self-indulgent to their wants.

Unhealthy:

Level 7

Ashamed

Fours are ashamed of themselves when their plans fail. They get depressed and alienate from the world so they don't have to see what they should have been.

Level 8

Contempt

They are surrounded in a personal hell, being tormented by their thoughts. They blame others around them for their failure and drive away those who try to help.

Level 9

Despair

Unhealthy Fours are prone to emotional breakdowns. They begin to feel hopeless, finding addictions to help them escape their personal torment.

Chapter 16: The Achiever

Synopsis

Top achievers of the general public, they live to attain to and accomplish, they should! These individuals are never content with average quality and they will do whatever it takes to sing the melody of triumph!

This part discusses:

• What an achiever is about

• Why are achiever great to have around

• What is most troublesome about achievers

• Dealing with them and drawing out the best

• Who they coexist with

• Who they don't alongside

Championing the reason for achievement, adoring an achiever for his or her exclusive expectations is the way to comprehension these people. Simply don't detract their heavenliness minutes from them and they will sparkle like a falling star coming to more noteworthy statures!

What Is An Achiever?

Achievers are creatures who live for approval. They will do whatever it takes to accomplish achievement, riches, acclaim, or anything that will get the consideration of their group.

They are the sorts that are dedicated, focused, endeavoring and cherishes elite difficulties and remunerates, for example, top deals, best division or even the most noteworthy score in a feature amusement.

They are additionally outgoing, have high vitality on account of the way they exhibit themselves, love their pictures of achievement and will never back up for fear that they be marked as a 'washout'.

The Good

An achiever lives for the objective – or the trust of accomplishing one. Due to their fundamental longing to create the impression that they are of quality to themselves, others and society, they will take a stab at the outcomes no matter what.

The best thing about them is that they take a stab at truthfulness — extraordinarily direct, they will get down to business or slice through all the smokescreens to get down to reality whether in life, wellbeing, religion or whatever other matter.

Driven, fearless and exceptionally commonsense, their vitality rouses individuals around them to work harder and they will ascend through the positions as they are great networkers also.

The Bad

The most noticeably bad thing about an individual in this state is that think that it difficult to be hint with other individuals.

They obsession with looking "great" makes it hard for them to be genuinely helpless which can be baffling for accomplices.

Where it counts inside, they are dishonorable for not being 'sufficient' to others — which will frequently lead them into making a false picture that isn't valid to themselves.

Achievers are focused on vanity – regularly satisfying everyone to keep up their picture and are prone to being deceitful.

Instructions to Deal With Them

To coexist with an achiever, you must help them to evacuate their essential trepidation of uselessness – always advising them that they are essentially of worth to everybody.

Sparing toward oneself achievers are ordinarily forlorn attaining to sorts in light of the fact that they won't impart their shortcomings so you will need to fill in for them when you know they are missing however not telling them what you did in light of the fact that they would prefer not to show up in need.

Sexual achievers must have comprehension accomplices who approve their self-esteem all the time by recognizing their prosperity, whether enormous or little. It is vital to understand that they need to seem fruitful and offering/giving to their mates as that is a feeling of their accomplishment.

Social achievers must be recognized openly. Whether by winning rivalries or elite circumstances, be their backing to see them win.

Verify they don't give others a chance to see them when they lose.

They work extremely well with supporters (sort 6) who are faithful to them and encourages their sense of self of achievement and they detest being around peacemakers (sort 9) who incline toward offering into average quality over shaking the standard of individuals keeping in mind the end goal to take a stab at brilliance or achievement.

Chapter 17: How Does Enneagram Personality Type Help Transform Your Life?

Now that you know more about meanings behind different personality types, you're probably wondering how it can actually help you. The main goal of knowing your personality type is to discover yourself, understand inner mechanisms, and constantly evolve or develop in every aspect of your life.

How can Enneagram help me develop?

Enneagram is your ticket for self-discovery and development through awareness. As mentioned throughout this book, Enneagram personality is identified through inner patterns i.e. those associated with your motivation, thoughts, and ways you respond in different circumstances. Sometimes we aren't aware of these patterns because they seem so natural to us. This is where the

Enneagram steps in. It provides a thorough analysis of your personality type and helps you become more aware of your emotions, needs, and thoughts.

Awareness is vital for change. If you're unaware of your automatic predictable behaviors and the effects they have on your life, how would you know what to change and how? By providing a deep insight into your psyche and every aspect of your character, the Enneagram allows you to determine your strengths and weaknesses. That way, you know what to work on in order to succeed, become happier, or achieve a certain goal. This is how you develop and make a progress consistently.

Your Enneagram personality type shows where you usually get "stuck" or pinpoints common struggles you face as well as your fears. Basically, it reveals all the mechanisms that drive you and it becomes easier to understand your inner patterns. With the Enneagram, it is easier to understand why we experience some hardships, but at the same time, you are more equipped to overcome them. For example, if you can't let go of negative experiences from the past, it could be easier when you understand your Enneagram type. How? That's because it shows why you feel that way and instead of denying your emotions and suppressing them, you develop more compassion towards yourself. Knowing the causes behind emotions, both positive and negative, enables you to process them in a healthy manner. This is yet another way the Enneagram helps you develop.

Probably the greatest advantage of the Enneagram in self-growth is its objectivity. Your personality type has both virtues and flaws. Every person has them, it's impossible to be perfect. That being said, sometimes we aren't objective and tend to criticize ourselves too much. Plus, sometimes you come across as arrogant or bossy even though it's not your intention. Being misunderstood is a common occurrence and it doesn't only depend on other people's perception of us. It also stems from the way you perceive others and yourself. The Enneagram helps you have a detailed insight into your personality in an objective manner. You become more aware of both virtues and flaws, which is a great way to become a more compassionate, successful, loving, person or to achieve any goal you have.

While some people are confident and learned to love themselves, others didn't. The greatest enemy that prevents us from succeeding in life is lack of love for yourself and Enneagram helps you solve this problem too. Only by understanding, you love something, and your own personality is not an exception. The more you understand yourself and the inner patterns implicated with feelings, thoughts, or relationships, the easier it gets to practice self-love.

The Enneagram also encourages you to be active in every aspect of life. What does this mean? Sometimes we are passive and expect things to just happen or we are afraid of failure and it seems logical to just wait and see what's going to happen. Life doesn't work that way. Every individual creates their own success and happiness. Every personality type achieves that success in a different way, depending on those inner patterns, but Enneagram encourages all of you (regardless of the type number) to take action and improve the ability to have a harmonious life. Here, the word harmonious can mean something different for any personality type, but the point is that you won't sit back and wait for things to happen, you become more proactive. With the newfound ability to achieve that, you get an additional opportunity to evolve and reach the perfect image of yourself.

Different ways knowing personality type improves your life

The Enneagram dissects an individual's personality and allows us to take an objective look at inner patterns. Since we're able to identify both strengths and weaknesses, we get an opportunity to develop in all aspects of life. If you're still wondering how it is possible to improve your life with the help of personality type, this will help you. Here are different ways you get to improve your life just by knowing whether you're Type One, Five, Six, or any other:

· Embracing your full self – what the Enneagram can teach is that everything about your personality is interconnected. You cannot be confident in your strengths without being aware of your weaknesses. When you know your personality type it gets easier to embrace your full self

· Helps narrow focus – you are drawn to the things that suit your personality the best. Sometimes we are confused and it becomes difficult to find a true passion. A specific personality type defines each individual and allows you to finally understand what you want to do or experience

· You're not alone – there are more than eight billion people in the world and we still feel all alone sometimes. We have both good and bad times, experience success and failures, love and want to be loved, but there always comes the time when you feel like nobody understands you. Just by reading the description of your personality type (or someone else's) you get the sense of belonging and realize you're not alone. There are many other people who are going through the same things

· Becoming less judgmental – although the best thing about our planet is its diversity, we've all judged someone because they didn't think or do things our way. Instead of trying to hide this fact, the healthy thing to do is to acknowledge it and find a way to solve the problem. The Enneagram personality helps you accomplish that. Knowing your personality type is a great way to understand yourself and why you judge others. At the same time, reading about other types allows you to understand their motivation and you become less judgmental when you consider some subject from their point of view

· Teaches you to trust yourself – we all hear a wide range of tips and advice for a better life. While there's nothing wrong with those, it is time to admit that one size fits all rule can't apply here. Different people require a different approach in every aspect of life. That's why it's important to trust yourself and your own ability to do great things in life. Personality type helps you filter people's advice through your set values. That way, you learn what you can from others, but stay true to yourself at the same time

Chapter 18: Type Five: The

Knowledgeable Caregiver

In This Chapter:

It is all in your head

I heard you the first time Of course I love you

Intimacy - Let's learn something together

Identifying the Five in Yourself and Others

Fives can be one of the easier types to pick out of a crowd, particularly if they're engaged in conversation, when their primary focus is on knowledge sharing and listening. Gestures are more limited and there's little, if any, small talk. There can be a detached quality, particularly in men, that seems removed of heart or feeling. Though often alone, the Five's social time is spent with knowledge oriented groups.

Nonverbal cues

Fives offer fewer nonverbal cues than other types. They gesture less frequently, and when they do, their gestures are often around the head area, where the type's excitement is expressed.

Other nonverbal cues of the Five are: Dressing for ease more than fashion.

Staring when listening but with minimal eye contact when talking. Particularly male Fives can seem like walking, talking heads.

Many are thin, feeding the mind more than the body. Missing or being oblivious to important social cues.

verbal cues

Fives tend to talk about what they are learning—financial services, contraindication of medications, estate law—subjects that might be over your head, and they can also be intellectual innovators. Listen well when they talk as they won't repeat themselves. They are skeptical, on average, yet if the information seems accurate and provable, Fives may explore astrology, psychic awareness, and esoteric arts.

Fives also:

Have a fairly quiet style, generally responding to questions rather than offering personal information.

Have a neutral voice tone, though it rises with excitement about an interesting topic of learning.

Have a sophisticated though succinct use of language. Can be dismissive of non-intellectual conversations.

Teach only what they know and are not instant experts.

Typically talk less than other types, though they can talk your head off on topics of interest, particularly if you seem receptive.

Fives in Caregiving

Detached, objective, analytical, and rational, Fives don't want to be overwhelmed with feelings, personal sharing, or high expectations from others. As knowledge seekers par excellence, they spend much of their time researching subjects for a depth of understanding.

Fives crave the learning experience. When you were a kid, did you tear things apart just to see how they worked? Are you doing the same now, studying the cause-and-effect factors in your Loved One's health? Do you see yourself as an observer now, wondering what is really true? If objectivity defines your approach, and you tend not to take things personally, you likely are a Five.

If you are a Five, you are reflective, and like the feeling of control that comes with understanding. You are more able than some others to think about your Loved One's life and medical needs without getting too emotional. Innovations, new perspectives on old ideas, or combining ideas or fields of interest to create new realities, are your cup of tea. You use your brain's creative power to unfold new possibilities and then test them with as much proof or logic as possible. You are rational and don't fall prey to whimsical thought or personal impulses, though your growth includes trusting your intuition as information.

Five's Positive Traits

Rational - You lean toward objectivity, which can help you to cope with the more traumatic moments. When circumstances become irrational and beyond your control, you can always revert to learning. You bring a solidness and rationality to your Loved One and family that can be calming in the face of trouble. You are reliable—if there is an answer to be had or a medical condition to be understood, you are the one to count on.

Innovative - While you approve of tried and true methods, your openness to new approaches may be a great help to your Loved One as you find new options for health and happiness. There's a lot to learn now, so keep up the curiosity and have the courage to face new ways of learning that are even more challenging.

Systems Thinkers - Since science beckons you, and technology is your playing field, you can easily take to understanding the healthcare system and the latest geriatric research.

Boundaries - You have better boundaries than most as you protect your personal space and don't dump your personal concerns or emotions onto others. You respect privacy, yet listen if others want to share. What a gift! You aren't swamped by emotions, which gives you an independence that doesn't require as much nurturing by others. You see others buffeted by the storms of personal reactions, and you want to make life work better. You are a calming mainstay as a caregiver.

Open to the Dark Side - One of Five's greatest assets is that they don't mind exploring the dark side of life. You are fascinated by everything. You can be curious when others shy away. Violence, medical prognoses, family dynamics? Fascinating!

Learn from Emotions - Fives don't get caught in emotional reactivity, though inner emotions can get stirred. At their best, Fives use their strengths to explore emotions and don't mind the confusion, fear, overwhelm, or uncontrolled feelings that accompany these times. They observe emotional states and learn from them. What do they represent? How can I change them?

Five's Challenges

Expressiveness - To some extent, average Fives disconnect emotionally from social needs, emotional states (such as fear, insecurity, and rejection), and the general tribulations of caregiving. When you do recognize emotions in yourself, your tendency is to not react, and you don't give many clues as to what's happening inside you. You give few signs of pleasure or agreement, though you may merely be checking things out and playing your cards close to the chest. If other family members are hyper-sensitive at this time they can easily misread you.

Intimacy - Intimacy can be a great challenge for a Five. While most people seek greater connection at this time, you may feel uncomfortable connecting with others' emotional expressions, and instead maintain an objectivity that can make you seem to be emotionally unaffected. Though you know that you care, others may not see the signs of your caring or concern and may pull away. The resulting emotional isolation

from loved ones is extremely painful, and hard to recover from without greater access to the language of emotion.

Rationality - Though your rational abilities present a great contribution, living too much in the rational realm at this time is a handicap. Compartmentalizing life into mental boxes creates an artificial separation between the many intricately connected aspects of caregiving, bypassing the potential heart and richness of your experience as it is informed by spirit and intuition.

Physical Isolation - Distancing protects you from pain, from revealing needs, and from feeling too attached to others, but it may hamper your ability to be effective. Yes, it is normal for many a Five to withdraw. Your study and research do require isolation, and what a perfect excuse! More to the point, if you have a limited facility for handling emotions, isolation can be desirable. But beware of protecting your private self at the expense of caregiving relationships and competency.

Five's opportunities for Personal Growth

You grow by extending yourself beyond the mind. Reveal more of your personal self, and live also in your body and heart. Feel completely your attachments to others and those feelings that well up inside. Express yourself in nonverbal ways. Give hugs, smiles, and your time. In order to

grow, take these steps:

Communicate - Begin in even small ways to put your feelings into words with trusted others. You might start by journaling to get more comfortable with this level of awareness. As you identify and share your feelings you will likely find that others draw closer to you. Your presence of both mind and heart can now bring you fully into the caregiving circle.

Connect with Yourself and Others - Make this your top priority, your next essential area of learning. Study your own disconnection and the cost to your relationships, and actively look for ways to be more connected, both with yourself and with others.

Explore Relationships and Emotions - The greater your ability to experience and navigate emotions the better support person you will be. A facility in the emotional realm can balance your given facility in the intellectual realm, making you a superb caregiver.

Require Solitude - In order to stay balanced you absolutely need some private time to regroup. Set up your life to have free time to look closely at all the learning that is available (even from the chaos of relationships, conflict, and stress) but don't get stuck in solitude. Be flexible, bearing in mind that with the immediate demands of care- partnering, you may at times need to act first and reflect later.

Be more expressive - People often misread you, because your hands or facial expressions don't correspond with your words. In fact, you often feel more than you are expressing. You tend to hold everything in, or speak in a neutral tone. Move out of fear and amplify your voice to show some emotion. Express your feelings, whether it's to get upset, or to tell those special to you how much they mean to you.

Make some small talk - Much as you may hate small talk, at times it is necessary when connecting to people. Talk more about what happened at the office, what you are thinking, what you had for lunch, and your next trip. Believe it or not, some people want to hear it! And when others are sharing, you needn't feel you have to tolerate inane conversations for an eternity. You can change the subject, request additional interesting information, change the subject, or just hang in there until the conversation becomes more substantive.

Feel your emotions - Sometimes it is just not possible for understanding to come first. You have to feel the emotions of sadness, fear, pain, anger, and joy, before you can understand them. Ride with emotional surges and conflicting desires and allow the understanding to come after. Keep a journal about your feelings. You'll find you can be more compassionate with others who focus on feeling.

Learn from doing - It is valuable to learn by diving into an experience and knowing you won't be perfect at it. Don't think before you leap!—jump in without knowing what you are doing, giving yourself permission to fall short. Let yourself be uncomfortable for a while. This is just one more opportunity to learn.

Go for love. You tend to spend a great amount of time alone. And yet nowadays, others may be calling on you for more connection. Allow yourself to enter the fray of relationships - attachment, belonging, and risk-taking. Express yourself to others. Cry and laugh. These times may painful, wonderful, confusing, and exhilarating, and it is life.

Consider new forms of knowledge. Open yourself to the many types of learning and wisdom - physical, emotional, spiritual, intuitive. Go beyond your mind to learn, opening to intuition or the psychic realm. Use music, theater, or mime to express parts of yourself that live outside rational frames.

Five's Heart, soul, and Mind

The average Five speaks and acts mainly from their learning mind and so may appear to be far less emotional, connected, or spiritual than others.

Fives in Relationships

It is rare to find a codependent Five—you can seem healthier than most. You appear not to be overly attached to others, nor do you expect others to compensate for your limitations. However, you can go too far by completely steering away from messy emotions in relationship. Especially during caregiving, relationships expose irrationality, projections, misunderstanding, and at times, chaos. If you respond by distancing yourself to study the situation, some others can feel rejected. At the same time, you may also hide your own needs, even from yourself, and can feel out of control if your desire, fear, anger, sadness, or joy becomes too strong.

It makes sense that relationships can be often awkward for a Five. Adept at learning from the mind, you may not pick up body cues or the complexity of social cues, or be able to read others' preferences, defensive states, or hidden meanings. People who are more difficult to understand may reject you or be upset when they feel misread. You may understandably respond by feeling overwhelmed or angry when their expectations make no sense or seem too much.

Most importantly, if you live too much in your mind, you can miss meeting other goals in caregiving, such as fully supporting your Loved One, healing family relationships, and preserving the family unit. Good relationships require time, shared experience and communication about differences.

As a Five your saving grace is that you can listen, and often listen well. You gather information that others likely miss, and listening is, of course, safer than sharing. You'd often rather have others lead the discussion. When you do give critical analysis and feedback it is often useful, but be careful not to be too blunt in your responses so that others can hear you. A soft approach is more easily heard.

Relationship Advice - So why expose yourself more than you are to the world of emotions? Unfortunately there's no way around it—this is a highly emotional journey. In normal times it is hard work for a Five to come out of your private space and into relationship. But now, to give your best support, you will need to make yourself available to the heart of caregiving. A Five's privacy and stoicism can be torture for other enneatypes that thrive on revelation and emotional depth, and without more input from you, others will only try to guess what is going on for you. Share your process as it is happening.

Five's Spiritual side

Fives are skeptics, and represent the highest percentage of agnostics or atheists of all the types. However, they respect the universe and are awed by the possibilities of studying it. Constantly curious, Fives integrate disciplines, analyze and classify, and develop theories of how the universe works. Fives ask the big questions and are always seeking the answers. Eventually their questions can bring them, in a roundabout way, to God—quantum physics now shows that there is a force far bigger than any of us which cannot be perfectly analyzed. The big questions about origins and deeper levels of reality were all invented by Fives of course. Fives are natural philosophers, creating frameworks for understanding the nature of reality. The mystery is constantly being revealed and understood. As a Five caregiver, your fascination for the mystery may help you to connect with your Loved One in their exploration of their own spirituality, which can be a great support to them, helping them to live with this challenging time of life. Perhaps you can explore together your beliefs and experience.

A Spiritual Lesson - If your Loved One has a faith or spiritual life that is different from yours, yet you have a rational awareness of a higher power, look for the ways in which their understanding can fit within

yours. Look for the points of potential spiritual connection between the two of you. Be accepting, for their sake if not for yours.

How Fives Think & Make Decisions

Fives are more interested in their learning process than in what to eat, what to wear, or the details of daily life. This can be a challenge or an opportunity when caregiving requires tending to the mundane details of life.

A Five pursues deepening knowledge about current reality. Her mind focuses on new pathways and discoveries. In caregiving, there are so many! One of a Five's greatest contributions is the understanding and researching of medical and life management information and options. Others may be swept away by emotional realities, but the Five comes through, keeping the family grounded in the practicalities. You serve as a counter-balance to their emotional focus, as you address the equally necessary realm of practicalities.

Decision-making for Fives is an exercise in careful consideration and logical analysis of all options. You don't want to be rushed. Once you've processed everything, you'll arrive at an independent decision. There's no place for personal desires and agendas, so you distrust others' input. You keep your head, listen to constructive feedback, and don't swing from one emotional pole to another. Your objectivity can be useful in a crisis, though your style can undermine your connection with others.

Ordinarily, a Five's inner thoughts might include:

I can't stand being around people who aren't smart. I want to get away from highly emotional people.

I wish there was more free time to research this topic. I wish I didn't have to sleep. I'd rather keep learning. Small talk is boring.

Five's Thought/Action Alternatives

As much as you can play a much-needed and valued role on a caregiving team, if you don't step beyond that role you risk missing a

lifetime opportunity to learn relationship skills. The more you can open yourself to this unfamiliar realm, the fewer will be your later regrets, and the stronger will be your relationships in the long run.

Try thinking the following and see where it takes you:

People are smart in different ways. Maybe I can learn from someone who is physically or artistically talented.

The mind isn't everything. People express themselves emotionally too. Maybe I can learn from this.

I can research by asking people questions or engaging directing in the topic, beyond reading.

Having enough sleep and eating healthy food can help me learn more!

Small talk is part of how people socialize. I'll start with that and shift toward a deeper conversation.

Making the Most of Being a Five

Five's playful Stress Type and masterful Growth Type offer moderation to Five's seriousness or lack of connection.

Five's stress Type - The Playful seven

Growth Type - The In-charge Eight

When Fives are stressed for a period of time, their thinking scatters like a Seven as they sample a bit of everything, jumping from activity to activity, but not tending to go very deeply into anything. They feel ungrounded, are easily distracted, and can't make decisions. Subjects change quickly. It is not so much a brainstorm as a brain tornado. The positive side of Seven can be developed too, offering more playful experiences without having to get too lost in thinking. Have a good time, laugh, and be silly. Fives can seem serious with study and the move to Seven can lighten things up.

The Growth Type for Five is Eight, the In-Charge, a powerhouse

type that is direct with communication, impulsive in actions, and trusting of their animal instinct, all good traits for Five to develop. It is good to balance your brilliant mind with body intuition, to act from your natural feeling, trusting that you'll figure it out along the way. You don't need so much preparation.

Your Eight integration protects you from mental obsessions, drives you to be more in your body (play sports, listen to what your body needs, eat well, exercise), and gives you permission to be more spontaneous. You will be more powerful, your ideas will have more of a punch, and you will speak with more determination and strength. Some Fives are very Eight-like in general, more direct than other Fives, and can have a heavier body build like some Eights.

Five's Wings - The unique Four & The cautious six

The two wings for Five are a Four wing (Five/Four) and a Six wing (Five/Six). Five's wings offer useful variety within the type, one bringing greater emotion and the other more systemic thinking.

Fives with the stronger Four wing can be more individualistic, preferring to have a touch of creativity, emotional awareness, and self- reflection in the process of living. If this is your wing, you like to be on your own, creating projects and mental worlds that have your own personal flair. Both the Five and Four are individualists and don't fit into any traditional mode. You listen to your own drumbeat, creating books, science projects, art projects, or nature-oriented learning with a flavor of feeling and panache. Downside? Operating on your own, you may not get the feedback you need to be an effective caregiver.

Fives with a strong Six wing are more strategic, more systemic in their thinking process, are less about their own individuality and are more interested in forwarding knowledge about how systems work. You take a broader sweep when sharing what you see. You explore the ways in which the minds of family members work, you use computers to extend your learning, and, as a researcher, study the interconnectedness of aspects of caregiving. Downside? You can be detached, so make sure your study includes a personal, people element.

Five's Degrees of Balance

Well-balanced Fives use their hearts as well as their minds, and are attuned to the body. They engage in life rather than withdrawing and detaching, and have learned to explore problems. They trust intuition as well as analysis. They are giving and nonjudgmental. They understand that intellectual ability is only one aspect of smarts. Everyone has a unique set of gifts and theirs extends beyond the mind. Knowledge extends to wisdom.

Average Fives struggle between feeling apart and including themselves in the world. Analyzing and categorizing life through mental concepts takes priority over involvement in life. The average Five can be open to new ways of thinking, as long as there's proof the new ways have validity. Relationships can be compartmentalized and distanced, and emotions repressed. The Five's heart needs to deepen while allowing herself to be affected by the need for connection.

Out-of-balance Fives tend to isolate themselves, living in their own private mind worlds, not getting much feedback.

Other people can seem strange, with their petty concerns and need for power. These Fives try to be competent in their special fields of knowledge but don't necessarily share their competence. The world can seem like a dangerous place, and Fives can isolate further, possibly wanting to connect, but not being able.

Chapter 19: Outline

Achievers are top entertainers who live for the approval of others. They cherish the lime light and they will do whatever it takes to achieve achievement, riches, notoriety, or anything that will get the consideration of their group. They are the sorts that are persevering, focused, endeavoring and adores elite difficulties and compensates, for example, top deals, best division or even the most astounding score in a feature amusement.

Themed the one-of-a-sorts, the maverick is an individual who flourishes as being totally novel to whatever remains of humankind. They are exceptionally unsure about their uniqueness and are creatures of unfathomable imagination in light of the fact that they are unique in relation to others. They detest the ordinary, standard and anything that is regular. Profound masterminds and analyzers, they are the rationalists of life and they have a solid enthusiasm for expressions, regardless of the fact that they don't end up to end up specialists.

Entertainer, Motivator,

Achiever, Producer or Status Seeker

They are additionally outgoing, have high vitality as a result of the way they show themselves, love their pictures of achievement and will never back up keeping in mind that they be marked as a 'failure'. Frequently the chameleon, they can here and there seem "fake" particularly when their essential obsession of vanity and picture love is showed. They experience issues separating themselves from a person versus a 'human doing'.

It's no shock that their blessed thought is trust. They are continually undertaking new tasks being driven by the need to attain to or "get" something new. At the point when one venture is done, they plan to attain to something else in their new venture.

Their biggest apprehension is uselessness – the powerlessness to be able in circumstances.

They yearning to be of quality to others on the grounds that they frequently characterize their self-esteem as far as honors and renown.

Their greatest enticement is to attempt and please everyone. Since their lives are characterized by the desires of others, society, or the achievement driven society, they have a tendency to bargain who they genuinely are getting to be mechanical and emotionless during the time spent their interest. Their most noteworthy bad habit is double dealing. This trickiness does not imply that they are inside and out liars yet it implies that they are the individual that will submerge themselves in the part they are playing to get a certain outcome. As such, their 'human doing' side of them shows so emphatically that the performing artist turns into the part they are playing.

Notwithstanding, the sort ones are taking care of business when they figure out how to be genuinely legitimate and truthful to themselves – recognizing their center goals and restoring their trust.

Sorts threes with a wing of two tend to be amazingly enchanting and supportive. They generally need to appear like the ideal mate, guardian or companion. Sort threes with a wing of four are by and large less picture cognizant, can have illusions of self importance and longings more imaginative results.

Nonconformist, Artist, Over-Analyzer,

Spiritualist or Melodramatic Elitist

They are tastefully touchy, exorbitantly sentimental and they cherish everything about translation toward oneself, exposure toward oneself or divulgence toward oneself... regularly offering their incredible discoveries to others and giving a solid commitment to the world. They additionally show themselves as exceptionally irritable and saved individuals particularly when their essential obsession of despairing is showed.

Their blessed thought is looking for their actual birthplace. They are the individuals who won't stop until they find their actual self — frequently driving profound into their feelings to take in more and all the more about themselves.

Their biggest apprehension is to seem basic. They despise the ordinary, the routine and the customary, liking to be over the standard.

They seek uniqueness and validness. They will do anything to feel uncommon, exceptional and they crave credible and genuine correspondence with others ⍰ regularly detesting the façade of fakery.

Their greatest allurement is censure toward oneself and withdrawal. When they feel deficient or doing something incorrectly, they have a tendency to pummel themselves steadily and withdraw from the frightening outside world.

Their most prominent bad habit is envy as they are dependably continually wanting what others have suspecting that their lives are so impeccable or complete (because of them imagining that they are never finish).

They are taking care of business when they take in the specialty of composure – by grasping the force of now and tolerating the occasion... getting a charge out of each delighted snippet of it.

Sort fours with a wing of three are regularly more noble type of elitism – the more outgoing of the nonconformist sorts while fours with a wing of fives are more withdrawn, mind boggling, examining and live in a private mythology of agony and misfortune.

Conclusion

Successful self-development occurs when we understand our inner patterns, determine strengths and weaknesses, but it also depends on fostering healthy and strong relationships with other people. The Enneagram helps us improve relationships in different aspects of our life in more ways than one.

From the very moment of birth, you are in a relationship (parents, siblings, other family members, friends, romantic parents etc.). Most people usually wonder what personality type suits them relationship-wise, but as mentioned earlier in the book, even though some types share similarities all of them are compatible with one another. The Enneagram is not like zodiac and doesn't help you improve relationships by suggesting you should engage with people who belong to the certain type.

When you understand your personality type it means you are aware of the inner patterns, motivations, desires, fears, virtues, and flaws. This means you understand where you're coming from. For example, a person who is Type Five understands what they seek in relationships with other people, but you also get an insight into how they perceive you.

By getting educated about other personality types, one finds it easier to understand their desires and what those people are looking for in different relationships. What can this teach you? Compromise! The key to a healthy relationship is a compromise. After all, the relationship isn't a dictatorship where one person is superior to the other and only they make all the choices. Both people in that relationship, romantic, platonic, family, should be equal and feel free to be open about their desires and what they expect from the other person. The Enneagram teaches you how to be confident, but still, accept other people's opinions and it are a great tool to improve every relationship in your life.

The opportunity to understand inner patterns of other people and compare them to yours helps you establish a deeper connection with others. This is the type of connection we are unable to achieve unless we understand ourselves and other people. It's like a domino effect because it's impossible to understand other people without knowing yourself. See, everything is connected, which is why the Enneagram is represented as a circle showing that although all nine personality types are different, they are strongly involved with one another.

Some people are open about their emotions, others aren't. Some of us are easily offended, but others are not. Plus, some people give love and want to be loved while others are confused and don't know how to express themselves the best way. All of us have different approaches to any type of relationship, but you always get puzzled. Why do people react/demand/feel certain things the way they do? Their Enneagram personality type explains it in detail. Learning how they react prevents you from taking them the wrong way or judging them.